MW00898096

LOOK INSIDE OF ME!

**Allowing the Spirit of God to search you
and direct your pathway**

By Timothy Wiebe

XULON PRESS

Copyright © 2007 by Timothy Wiebe

Look Inside of Me!
Allowing the Spirit of God to Search You and Direct your Pathway
by Timothy Wiebe

Printed in the United States of America

ISBN 978-1-60477-236-4

All rights reserved solely by the author. The author guarantees all contents are original and do not infringe upon the legal rights of any other person or work. No part of this book may be reproduced in any form without the permission of the author. The views expressed in this book are not necessarily those of the publisher.

Unless otherwise indicated, Bible quotations are taken from the New King James Version (NKJV). Copyright © 1982 by Thomas Nelson, Inc.

www.xulonpress.com

CONTENTS

Dedication vii
Introduction...ix
  1. God Knows You 11
  2. Search Me Oh God..23
  3. Going Deeper...31
  4. Meeting My Wife 49
  5. Life and Ministry Growth 57
  6. Full Time Ministry 65
  7. 11 Years In Merkel, Texas...........................75
  8. When the Holy Spirit Visits You 107
  9. Becoming Recharged and Renewed 113
10. Hearing and Knowing God's Direction 119
11. Love Is the Key 127
12. Finding the Secret Place with God..............135
     Biography...147

DEDICATION

I praise God for His grace and strength in helping me to write this book. I dedicate it first to you Lord.

To Rebekah, my wife, I love you so much. Thank you for supporting me, for standing beside me, for never letting go of hope, for being the love of my life, and my best friend. You are the joy of my life in this world.

And to my children, daughter in law, and grand children, (Timothy and Summer, Sydney, Sadie, Preston), Phillip, and Rachel - Thank you for blessing me. Your strength, insights, love and encouragement mean more to me than I could ever express in words. I love you!

Thank you Harvest Church Family. Thank you for being genuine. Thank you for being patient and allowing me to take time to write, for your love, and for being so supportive and encouraging.

Thank you John Hansen, my dear friend, for going the extra mile, and taking the time to do all the editing.

INTRODUCTION

P eace, inner strength, compassion, ability to overcome sin, as well as knowing the actual desires of God for one's life are attributes that most Christians would like to walk in the knowledge of, yet it seems that so few come to find in great depth. My desire in writing this book is to explore what happens when a person allows the Spirit of God to look deep inside of them, allowing Him to have, not only a part in their lives, but also to trust Him to the place of opening up the depths of their soul to Him. I believe that in so doing, not only will great peace begin to flow within, as you've only dreamed of, but that you will begin to find great pleasure in life, and in the plans that God has for you. I believe that His searching of our hearts allows His will to be revealed in us. Throughout my lifetime, I've come to see the hand of God protecting and leading me, directing my steps and guiding me in business decisions, and many other life choices. I've witnessed Him giving me favor with people, disciplining me when I was drifting from Him, comforting me when I was hurt and bruised, and renewing my mind in the midst of chaos. I'm learning that no matter how much we've come to know the Lord, there is still much more to experience in Him as we humble ourselves, and seek Him diligently. Come join my quest. I believe that life ahead for you, and for me, will be more completely full of love and blessing than ever imagined, or thought possible, as we say with a broken spirit, and abandonment to Jesus, "Come Holy Spirit, look inside of me".

Chapter 1

GOD KNOWS YOU

There is nothing that the Lord doesn't know about you and I. He not only formed us, but He sees us, knows our thoughts, our struggles, and all that makes us tick. He knows what we enjoy, what we hate, what drives us, what motivates us, and where our passions lie. God also knows what lies dormant within us, what possibilities there are inside of us, and most importantly, He knows how to bring the best out of us. He has the absolute, perfect ability, by His Spirit to do miraculous things within and through us. His plan for us includes our lives being blessed beyond our comprehension.

(Eph, 3:20) Now to Him who is able to do exceedingly abundantly above all that we ask or think, according to the power that works in us…

Much of what God knows about us, and sees within us, I believe, are things that He desires to reveal to us. The way He has chosen to reveal those blessings to us is by our surrender and submission to His searching of our souls. We must open up to Him, surrender our will, and let go of unprofitable things, if we are to unlock the door to our potential in Christ. There are attitudes that we develop throughout our lifetime that may be destructive to our future, as well as hurts that we have suffered, that we have not been able to let go of by our own strength and ability. It may be helpful to look at where we've come from, in order to see where God desires to take us.

Who Was I?:

When I was 14 years old, I had an emotional addiction to marijuana and was also using just about any type of drug that I could get my hands on at the time. I was lonely, depressed, and completely without direction for my life. I had absolutely no idea that God had a plan for my life. I had no comprehension that He had a desire for me to not only know Him intimately, but also to share this love of His with thousands of others in the years to come. All I knew was, that I was lonely, depressed, discouraged, without friends, and feeling that life for me was going nowhere in particular. My thoughts of myself were that I was no one special, without much to offer anyone else. Also I had the opinion that everyone around me was some-what better than me and that they were more capable of fitting in with society than I was. I was blinded to the blessings God had prepared for me because I had not yet opened up my soul to the searching of the Holy Spirit. His desire was to bring to fruition the healing and freedom that I was in desperate need of.

I didn't really know how to open myself up to Him. Although I had an encounter with Christ at age 9, as my Mother had lead me in the "Sinner's Prayer" in our living room, and was inundated with the presence of God at kid's camp, I didn't yet understand God's plan for me and how to stay close to Him.

I was raised as the youngest of 6 children, with one brother who was 12 years older than I, and four sisters sandwiched in between. My Father was a determined, dedicated businessman, who cared deeply for his family, and was committed to taking care of us in this world. He was raised on a farm in Canada, where life was hard. Real hard! He was raised in a Mennonite community, and in the understanding that children were to be seen and not heard. He shared many stories with me from his childhood, including being taken by his Father on long trips to other farms, and with nothing being said to him he would be left at the farm to work for the farmer for a month or so. This was the case with my Dad's brothers as well, and was a way of earning money to help support the household.

At age 13, my Dad left home and began going from town to town looking for work. Most of what he was able to earn he sent home to his Mother and Father. He lived on his own, taking odd jobs and hopping trains, until he met my Mother. My Dad's upbringing had created a tough exterior. At age 17, my Dad began working in a slaughterhouse, and learned to cut meat. This became his trade, and later in life allowed him to make very good wages in the grocery business. He became part owner of a grocery store, and later became a supervisor of the meat departments of over 30 A&P stores in the Midwest. His position with A&P took us to Chatham, IL. Because of my Dad's varying positions in the grocery business, we moved quite frequently.

I was born in Dearborn, Michigan. From there we moved to Montgomery Village, Maryland, then on to Chanhassen, Minnesota, and from there to Illinois, where my Dad began employment with the A&P Tea Company. I was 12 at the time. Because of the frequent moves, it seemed that I had not established an identity. I had never lived anywhere long enough to obtain long-lasting friendships. Because of always being the new kid in town, there was the scourge of that title hanging over my head, leading to continual run-ins with bullies, as well as those who would try to take advantage of my timidity and quiet nature. I had never felt truly accepted in any town where we had lived, or in any school I had attended.

I felt, in some ways, as though I was an only child. While my brother was 12 years older, and we had little in common, my sisters were (I felt) very popular, and into their own world, so to speak. In reality, I really didn't expect them to spend a great deal of time with me. They were my sisters whom I loved, but I had a great and natural desire to have my own personal friends. There was a feeling of rejection hanging over me, as I reflect now, that I had no clue of in those days.

My Dad's head office with his new job at A&P was in Springfield, Illinois, but he moved us to the small town of Chatham, because of his desire to keep me, and my sister Darlene, in a small town, and in a small school setting where there would hopefully be less temptation to get involved in drugs and alcohol. Nothing could have been further from the reality of the matter. As I began the first day of eighth grade, I walked into the lunch room, and saw all the "jocks" on one side, with their short hair, and all the long haired kids on the other side. I felt I needed to make a choice as to who to sit with. I had no friends, had moved quite frequently in my short lifetime, and was extremely shy, and timid. I had long hair, which was common at that time for those not involved in school sports, and so I went to that side. It took almost no time at all for me to realize that this school was full of drug users, and drug dealers, and I was sitting with them, with a great need to feel accepted. Pot was smoked daily, right behind the school building at the "smoking tree". Yes, there was a giant oak tree behind the school, where kids were permitted to smoke cigarettes. Much of what was being smoked, however, was marijuana, and I joined in. I'll never forget the morning that we were passing a pipe around, as we stood in a circle just outside the school's back door, when suddenly I noticed the principle stepping out to check on us. As he did, someone threw the pipe. The principle called my name, and asked me to follow him to his office. I did, and what ensued was life altering for me. In his office he said something like this: "Tim, I know that you are a good kid. I know that you don't want to be involved with those pot heads, and I called you in here to see what you can tell me about them." He wanted information from me, but I gave him nothing. I was not about to be considered a "nark", which would mean the end of what little social life I had at this school.

Everything Backfired

After that day, when the other kids saw that I had not been punished, they must have assumed that I had become an informant to the Principal. From that moment on, I became the scourge of those kids. They hated me with vehemence. Walking down any hallway in the school became a dangerous encounter. I was pushed, shoved, books were knocked out of my hands repeatedly, and I was thrown into a nearby lake. In addition to this I had pretty much lost every friend that I may have had.

Now on to ninth grade, still attending the same school and being punished by peers for simply attending classes, it became difficult to go on. I was made to shine the shoes of those much bigger and stronger, was threatened repeatedly, and was greatly misunderstood because of my quiet and timid nature. I could not go to the principal, as this would only worsen my fate, in my view. One night I attempted desperately to speak to my Dad about the situation. His response was overwhelmingly destructive to my spirit, though, looking back now, I can understand where he was coming from, as he lived through such a difficult childhood. His response was basically this, "Grow up!" "Are you gonna be a man or a little kid all your life?" At any rate, I knew that I would never ask him for advice on the subject again. My use of drugs, and alcohol increased quite a bit from that moment on, as well as staying out all night, and running away from home a time or two for short periods of time, as I felt desperate for acceptance and identity.

Because of the drug abuse and insecurity, I was failing in school badly. I was pretty much a straight F student, and accordingly was placed in a special education class and also assigned to regularly meet with a psychologist. The psychologist asked me who the Vice President of the United States was, and I didn't know. He actually had me putting square and round pegs into holes, which seemed like utter nonsense to me. Not long after, I intercepted a letter from our mailbox that was sent to my parents by the psychologist. It said this... "Tim sits with his head down, says nothing, does nothing, and sleeps on occasion." It went on to say that, in his opinion, I had done harm to my brain with drug abuse, and that I would more than likely never graduate from high school.

The Knockout Punch

One thing to keep in mind as you read this is that my brother was 12 years older than I, and was married and living in Michigan. I had one sister left at home, (Darlene), who had her own responsibilities, and difficulties. One day as I was entering my history class, two students, who had been pushing me around, approached me. I was not afraid of either one of them individually, but knew that I was up against more than one individual. Although I was shy and timid, there was another side to me that was very aggressive. That aggressiveness may have been the result of fear itself. Nevertheless, these two boys began pushing me right in front of my history teacher. I guess I felt somewhat secure with the teacher sitting close by, so I reacted. I shoved one of them to the floor. In the next moment I was recovering from a temporary blackout, as I lay on the floor. I then realized that I had been punched in the jaw. As I attempted to get up for a response, the kid sat on my chest, with his fist in my face, saying, "Get up, and I'll knock you right back down." The teacher looked on and did nothing. For the life of me, I could not understand that teacher's lack of response. I went to my chair and sat through the class, not paying attention to another word the teacher spoke. I sat through that class contemplating my future. I decided in that moment of time, that I would never again attend classes in that school, where no one seemed to care. When the class was over, I left the building, determined never to return again.

I felt very strongly that I could not tell my parents that I was not going back to this school, since I knew that would be unacceptable. Because of my situation, I began intercepting letters and phone calls left on the answering machine from the school. My parents both worked, so I was somehow able to keep them from finding out that I was skipping school. I skipped over 80 days of school that freshman year, and eventually the school officials quit calling and sending letters, assuming that we had moved away (as I found out later). In order to maintain my parents' trust that I was attending school, I would take the bus to school, but not attend. I would walk in the front door, and right out the back. There was a feeling of power in doing this, a feeling of taking control of my life, and yet I had no clear direction. My life was like a ship on a journey with no captain or overseer.

During this time I would also, regretfully, steal money from my Mother, in small amounts, to buy drugs. When I was out of money I would steal drugs, whenever possible. I had also made friends with a few "druggies" who were out of school, whom I would call, on many occasions from a payphone, for rides to their house from the school where I would hang out. One of those friends, lived two doors down from my house, and became my very best friend. Mike had his own car, always had pot, and loved to drink Little Kings Cream Ale. We did a lot of partying together, as he introduced me to other drug users all over Springfield, Illinois. On a few occasions we stole from each other, and yet still somehow maintained a friendship.

All through this time, I had the knowledge of the Salvation experience that I had had when I was 9 years old, and there were certain things that I would not do. One of those things was to take God's name in vain. Another was fornication. There were plenty of opportunities at the parties I was attending, and the temptations were many, but I literally feared the fire of hell as it relates to that part of my life because of the church upbringing and sermons I'd heard over the years. Because of the rejection by my peers, and the newfound older friends that were in my life, I was growing up in a hurry. The only problem was that these were not the older friends who would lead me in the right direction. They were thieves, drug users, and dealers, blasphemers, fornicators, and despisers of all that is good and just. One of these older "friends" gave me a bag of pot to sell, saying, "sell $30.00 worth, and smoke the rest." Instead of doing that, I smoked the whole bag. Afterward, he came to our front door, while were we eating as a family. He wanted his money. My Dad came to the door, and asked what he wanted, and he replied, "Your son owes me $30.00 that I loaned him." My Dad simply told him to get off of our property, and never return. My Dad knew that something was out of order, but I'm sure he didn't know what exactly to do, or really what was going on. I was very good at hiding my "drug" identity, and my parents seemed oblivious to it.

Not long after this, I met someone who was new in town. We drank a 12 pack of Budweiser together, and smoked some pot. As I recall, we were also taking other drugs of one sort or another. That night we broke into a bowling alley, attempted to steal a car, stole some bicycles, and accidentally burned down a building by setting wall posters on fire inside of it. A couple of days after this event, my parents sent me to church camp. This would become a life altering experience for me. One night during this camp, I ran to the altar, cried out to God, and was filled with the fire and overcoming power of God's Holy Spirit. My Dad picked me up at the church, and I exclaimed, "Dad, you'll never have another problem with me. My life has been changed by God." He was silent, and I thought that was very odd. After a short while, he said, "That is all good, son, but I have to tell you that the police are waiting for you at the house." My "friends" had told the police that I was the one they were looking for. I didn't really care. My life was changed, I knew it, and I wanted to tell the world, especially the police, who had chased me around Chatham and through the grave yard on more than one occasion.

When the police came in the house, they told me that I was not the one they were really after, but the young man that I had been running with was the most wanted criminal in Sangamon County. I had no idea of who this person really was that I had been running around with, and I had only just met him. I proceeded to tell the police everything I knew, including all that we had done, all the while telling them of my life changing experience at camp. The police seemed very grateful for my testimony, and these cops, who knew me well, acknowledged that I even looked different. At the same time, they told my parents and me that, because of my confession, I would be sent to a boys' home for a time. They said that they knew that I was different, but there was nothing they could do to change the law. When they left the house, my parents and I knelt down and prayed fervently that God, who had changed me, would spare me from this. To this day, I have never heard from any law enforcement agency concerning that situation and me. Those officers knew I was different, and God was beginning to show me His favor!

Chapter 2

SEARCH ME OH GOD

Psalm 139:7

7 Where can I go from Your Spirit?
Or where can I flee from Your presence?

VV 23-24

23 Search me, O God, and know my heart;
Try me, and know my anxieties;
24 And see if *there is any* wicked way in me,
and lead me in the way everlasting.

Salvation is the beginning of walking with God:

Although I had a salvation experience at a young age, I had no idea that I needed to continue opening myself up to God, and allowing Him to search me in order to unlock the potential that was there. Because of this lack of understanding, my relationship with God was somewhat distant. I knew that we were all sinners, who needed a Savior, but what I didn't know was that He greatly desired to manifest Himself within me and that He longed so greatly to know ME. My thoughts of salvation were somewhere along the lines of "Repent so that your sins will not be held against you, and you'll get to go to heaven when you die, you scoundrel." I didn't know that Jesus wanted to floor me with His presence, literally every day. I didn't know that He delighted in me, rejoiced over me with songs, and had great anticipation of simply meeting with me.

Zephaniah 3:17 (New International Version)

17 The LORD your God is with you,
   he is mighty to save.
   He will take great delight in you,
   he will quiet you with his love,
   he will rejoice over you with singing."

After all, who was I? I was nobody. He was King of Kings, and Lord of Lords. I knew this, because we sang songs about Him at church along those lines. I knew who He was, but I didn't know who I was. I didn't know that I was the "apple of His eye." I didn't know that He was lonely without a relationship with me. I didn't know that He wasn't interested in a relationship with "religious people," (Those who love religion instead of God) but simply people who greatly loved Him, and desired to know Him, and for Him to know them. I didn't realize that rules were not all that God was about, but rather love, and not just any kind of love, but a love that cannot be found in any fleshly, earthly thing. His love is one that is so deep that it surrounds a person, embraces a person, envelops that person, and then reveals to that person that they are only experiencing the very beginning stages of that love. The love of God is not a passive, inactive love, but rather a great living love:

Ephesians 2:4-5 (New Living Translation)
> 4 But God is so rich in mercy, and he loved us so much,
> 5 that even though we were dead because of our sins, he gave us life when he raised Christ from the dead. (It is only by God's grace that you have been saved!)

I had had my wonderful experience with God at Church Camp, but little did I know that this was only the beginning, and the best was yet to come.

Getting to Know God

After my glorious and life changing encounter with God, I was different. I had truly repented of my sin, by confession of it, and accepting the gift of Gods grace. What I did understand immediately was that His grace was His ability in me. That it was not my being good that could save me, but rather, the overcoming ability of His Holy Spirit living on the inside of me. I was completely in awe of this experience in my life at age 15. Now, attending church was not boring, it was joyful, happy, and exciting. The worship times were filled with splendor, because now the songs of worship had deep meaning for me.

They were no longer only songs sung about God, but songs sung to God, from our hearts, from the hearts of those who had this same life changing experience as I did. Suddenly I felt as though I was a part of the congregation, rather than a bystander, who wasn't accepted. Because God accepted me, I could now begin to see how other believers could accept me, and that they truly were my brothers and sisters in Christ, and that we were members of one another. I'll never forget my Youth Pastor, Mark Johnson, who had an immediate impact in my life. Although I had experienced the joy of salvation, I was still shy, timid, withdrawn to a great degree, and with no idea of how to fit in. We were attending a large, "full gospel" church in Springfield, Illinois. The Youth Minister was the Pastor's son, and there were approximately 300 in our youth group. The church had grown to the extent that they had built a new sanctuary onto the old facility, and the older part of the building became the youth sanctuary. The church's midweek service was on Thursday nights, and the youth group had its own service, complete with a full worship band, including talented musicians, and singers. The youth minister's dedication to teaching, and disciple-ship had an extreme impact on my life. I was not yet established in who I was, much less in how to fit into a large and vibrant youth group. Our youth minister took an interest in everybody, while at the same time, involving young people in ministry who seemed to have that calling, and desire. This had to be extremely difficult to do with so many youth. He taught us every week, about who Christ was and what place He wanted to have in our lives. He helped me to get involved and to become the person that God had called me to be. On many occasions, Mark would take us to nursing homes, as well as other towns, and other churches, and get us involved in singing, testifying, and preaching. I had become a part of a youth choir that had been started by Pastor M.C. Johnson's wife (Betty Johnson), called the "Transitions." Another group had been developed, that I had also become a part of called, "Lightening Bolt." We went to rock concerts handing out gospel tracks, and sharing the gospel on the streets, as well as at the hospital, and from door to door. Some would stay at the church making calls to those who hadn't been in church recently, and encouraging them in the Lord. Thirteen rented school busses were used each week to bus kids in for Sunday school, and we would go out on Saturdays to invite them.

THE NEW SCHOOL

At the start of what would have been my sophomore year of High School, my Mother took me to register at Chatham High School. After inquiring about whether I would be required to make up all of 9th grade, after missing most of the year, and failing every class. We were informed that the school was prepared to pass me on to the next grade, while placing me in a special education class. I was nervous. I now had a new found boldness in the Lord, but I was not comfortable with the idea of going back to this school, where so many negative things had taken place for me. At the same time, we had become aware that our church had started up a Christian School, so my Mother and I met with the principal, Donna Squires, who was the Pastor's daughter. Donna looked me in the eye and said with confidence, something to the effect of "We would love to have you to be a part of our school. I believe the Lord is leading you here. What do you think?" The only problem was that the school only went through 9th grade, and they would be adding a grade each year. There was no doubt within me that this was where God was leading me. To retake 9th grade didn't seem too big of a sacrifice, when comparing it with going back to my old school. I spent the next 4 years in the church's school, graduating with honors at the end of that 4 year period. I'll never forget thinking of how I wished that I could find that school Psychologist, the one who said I would likely never graduate from high school, and wave my diploma in his face.

During those school years, I grew in my knowledge and understanding of God. I came to know Him more dearly, and more personally, as each week went by. At age 16, while attending yet another church camp, in Carlinville, Ill. I found myself one night at an altar, praying, and hearing these words, as the Spirit of God spoke them to me..."I want you to preach my Word." I felt that I must be imagining this, because, giving a testimony was one thing, and was very nerve-racking in itself for me, I couldn't imagine standing in front of two people to preach, much less an entire congregation. But as I knelt there, I continued to hear those words within me. "I am calling you to preach my Word." It didn't take long for me to get up, and begin to head for the exit. I was distressed by what I felt in my spirit that night. The thing that was farthest from my mind in those days was becoming a preacher. As I approached the exit, a teenage girl approached me, and without hesitation, pointed her finger in my face, and said these words... "Don't you run away from the call of God. God is calling you!" In that moment, my knees hit the floor, right there in the middle of that auditorium, and I accepted the call of God on my life. Within the next few days, I shared this experience with my Youth Pastor, who in reply said something along these lines... "I know. I've sensed the call of God on your life." From that moment, I began to get more actively involved in leadership in the youth group, as well as in school. With permission from the school, I started a daily bible study at lunchtime. I would eat as quickly as possible and then rush upstairs to the school library, taking anyone who would come along. In those times, I would teach what I had been learning, as well as open up discussions. One young man, who would join us occasionally, was Jimmy Smith. Jimmy would end up being the first peer in my life to challenge me and keep me on my toes in my growing knowledge of the Word of God (thanks Jimmy) Those were very special times. Although I was involved in all that I could find to do, I was hungry for more of God.

Chapter 3

GOING DEEPER

In those teen age years, I was aware that the presence and power of the Holy Spirit was on my life and working within me, but I wasn't satisfied. I knew that there was something more, and that I must press into prayer to find a closer walk with Jesus. During altar times, following the preaching of our youth Pastor, I would stay at the altar, seeking God for more of Him. "I love you, Lord," I would say. "I need more of you. Show me more. Help me to tell others. Show me your ways. Fill me with your Spirit." I was so hungry for God. I wanted His presence. I longed to be near Him, and when I was sensing His presence, I didn't want to move. Many times, I would get up from the altar area, only to look around and find that most of the youth were gone. As a group, many times we would go to the local Godfathers Pizza, or just out cruising the town after church. I'll never forget the night that I was praying at the front, during altar time. One of my close friends was praying with me. His name was John Peters. John and I were next to each other, but praying separately, when we suddenly both became extremely lost in the presence of the Spirit of God, and this time there was something different happening. I was interceding for John, and he was interceding for me. I cannot fully describe this experience, but I can tell you that I became oblivious to my surroundings, as did John. Time passing by seemed as nothing, while we interceded for each other in the Spirit of Christ. As we finished praying, we looked at each other and I said, "Did what just happened to me, happen to you?" John looked back and said "yes! Did this happen to you?" We had been carried away in the Spirit of God, and had interceded for one another in a supernatural way, a way that cannot be fully explained in natural terms. I was beginning to discover the meanings of scriptures such as:

Ephesians 6:12 (New Living Translation)
12 For we are not fighting against flesh-and-blood enemies, but against evil rulers and authorities of the unseen world, against mighty powers in this dark world, and against evil spirits in the heavenly places.

I was learning to walk in the Spirit, and to find out the purpose God has for us in His Spirit. I was learning that walking in the Spirit and praying in the Spirit was not for the purpose of goose bumps and good feelings, but for the purpose of edifying, exhorting and interceding for others, as our lives become more full of the strength of God. He was revealing His Kingdom to me, as He desires to do in you, and in all of His children. I began to have a thirst for prayer that was absolutely unquenchable. In those days, it was not unusual at all for me to spend 1, 2 or even 3 hours in prayer at one time. Sometimes I would just lie on my back, weeping, and rejoicing as His Spirit washed over me. His love was inundating me. I could literally feel within me God saying, "I love you. I love you so much." I was learning that in order for me to help others to be free, I had to know the movements of the freedom of God inside of me in deeper and more intimate ways. I was discovering that God wasn't simply looking for a vessel to use to preach to others, but that He truly desired fellowship and communion with me. I was beginning to see that I was His beloved.

Song of Solomon 2:4 He brought me to the banqueting house, and his banner over me *was* love.

During those teen years, one thing that seemed to have stayed with me to some degree, from my former days, was the feeling of rejection by my peers. I had joined the basketball team at school, and was quick, practiced hard, and absolutely loved the game. My coach told my Dad that I had the most "potential" of anyone on the team. I soon discovered that having potential ability, a love for the game, and a drive to become better, would not earn me a spot in the starting rotation. I felt rejected by the other players on the team. It was a Christian school, but not necessarily all students were Christians, and I didn't fit in with some of the guys on the team. I didn't share their interests, wasn't a part of their circle of friends, and found that the basketball was not finding its way to me, even if I was standing wide open. The rejection I felt on the court stayed in my spirit during school hours as well, and my sorrow over this deepened. "God, when will people like me? Why do I have to be rejected my whole life? What is wrong with me?" Church leaders, as well as popular students, passing me in the hallways, would frequently say, "cheer up, smile, life isn't so bad." I didn't know that I wasn't smiling, and I didn't know how to improve on that, though I did try. I felt as though I was being monitored by the whole world. I also felt as though I just couldn't measure up to expectations, and that I would never be able to fit in with the "in" crowd. The most difficult part of this, was that my youth Pastor didn't seem to be able to relate to where I had come from, and what I was going through, and I didn't know how to, or if, I should approach anyone with my struggles with feeling unaccepted. As for the basketball team, I just became so angry, so hurt, and so confused, and felt that I couldn't take it any longer. One day I waited outside the building, after another game of sitting on the bench. I was waiting for coach to come out so that I could tell him "how wonderful he was."

I was really going to let him have it, and give him a piece of my mind. At that moment, I guess I thought he was about the cruelest person I knew. He didn't come out, and I went home. In retrospect, this coach must have been under stress to win. He was a very driven and dedicated man, and simply put, kids who know each other well, play together well. I told my Dad of my struggle, and how I was not getting any playing time. My Dad called the coach that night, and regretfully, took me off of the team. I would not have quit, but now I had to face everyone, including my coach who was also one of my teachers, feeling that I would be considered a quitter. That was my freshman year, and I never played high school basketball again.

My low self-image, along with the feeling of rejection, was the most difficult part of growing up. Being rejected by worldly kids was one thing, but feeling rejected by some of the popular church youth seemed more than I could bear. Looking back now, I can see how the Lord intervened, providing friends for me.

During my high school years, I became involved in drama class, even playing the part of the Pastor in a play held in the main sanctuary. I discovered that, although I was shy and timid, when I was acting I became a different person and able to release all that was in my personality. I would think of how God chose David, when no one else would have chosen him. Not even his own earthly father would have chosen

David. David was the loner, the kid out in the field, tending to the sheep, and singing songs. He was no warrior, and certainly not King material. But God sees what men do not see. God sees the heart. He sees, not what men see in you, but He sees what He has created you to be. He sees your potential in Him, and once a person opens up their soul to God, and to the searching of His Spirit, He begins to bring that person to a place of understanding and fulfilling of their God given dreams. He takes that surrendered person, and says, in essence, "I don't care what the world says of you. You are a fierce, mighty warrior. You are precious to me, and someone that I am raising up for my glory. Don't concern yourself with the rejection of men. Set your gaze upon me. Set your affection upon me. Set your hope and trust in me, and then look and see what I am about to do in your life."

In those teen years, along with my new desire for God, was a desire for companionship, the desires for dating, for human love, and affection. I had already experienced much drug abuse, alcohol abuse, along with the experience of betrayal, deceit, loss of friends, misunderstandings, etc. So I was very much interested, at a young age, in having a serious relationship with a Godly girl, someone who would hopefully place spiritual interests above carnal ones. Someone who would desire to discuss loving Jesus, and walking with God. This was what I most longed for in discussion in my relationships with others. There were lots of girls in our youth group, and I had my share of dating. I soon discovered that some of these girls were not Godly at all. Some of them were sensual, driven with passions, and not at all interested in discussing the things of God. In all fairness, I was older than most of the girls I dated, and they were pretty much just looking to have a good time. One girl I dated briefly was looking to escape the reality of a terrible home life. She told me that she hoped to get pregnant so that she could get out of living at home. Although I was just as tempted as the next guy, I couldn't imagine grieving the Holy Spirit, by allowing myself to fall into sexual sin, and frankly, I couldn't understand, for the life of me, how anyone full of God's love, could run into it full throttle without hesitation. I don't speak any of this condemningly as I have come to understand not only that anyone can fall under the wrong circumstances, but I've also come to understand that God's mercies are new every morning, and that there is no condemnation in Him when we turn to Him. I was no better than the next guy, but I was learning to keep myself in the midst of the favor of God, by His Spirit.

1 Corinthians 10:13 (New Living Translation)

13 The temptations in your life are no different from what others experience. And God is faithful. He will not allow the temptation to be more than you can stand. When you are tempted, he will show you a way out so that you can endure.

I was no "Mr. Innocent," but, because of the level of my relationship with God, and the infilling of the Holy Spirit in my life, I was just not happy with compromise, and indeed was being led by the Spirit in the direction of good things for my life that He had in store for me. I remember several occasions of driving home, after going no farther than kissing with a girl, and crying out to God all the way home, asking Him to forgive me. Jesus was so real to me and I didn't want to hurt Him. I couldn't bear to break His heart, and to grieve His Spirit. After all, I was free because of the working of His Spirit within me. Why would I jeopardize that liberty? During those years, I was experiencing the favor of God, without understanding fully what that meant. Little did I know that God doesn't simply say, "Thou shall not!" He also says, "I have life for you, and that abundantly." He says this:

Jeremiah 29:11-14 (New Living Translation)

11 For I know the plans I have for you," says the LORD. "They are plans for good and not for disaster, to give you a future and a hope. 12 In those days when you pray, I will listen.

13 If you look for me wholeheartedly, you will find me. 14 I will be found by you," says the LORD. "I will end your captivity and restore your fortunes. I will gather you out of the nations where I sent you and will bring you home again to your own land."

God's commandments are not grievous to us, particularly not as we walk in Christ Jesus. As we walk and live in Jesus, we walk under a covering of the blood of Christ, (applied by the Holy Spirit) and an anointing of the Spirit of God, who not only cleansed us once, but once and for all. His power, dwelling within us, is able to supply all the ability that we will ever need to overcome sin, as we abide in Him. Salvation is not only an experience of the supernatural only to leave a person living the rest of his life in the natural.

Now, humility, and surrender to Jesus are the driving forces behind the power that we have in Him. God is a responder. He responds to our faith. By faith, we act. By faith we seek after God, knowing that He is a "rewarder of those who diligently seek Him." God does not use us as vessels by force, but rather vessels of surrender. We are to be presenting ourselves to Him, as living sacrifices, not in the sense of attempting to justify ourselves before others, but in the sense of humility, and constant acknowledgement of our dependence upon Him. Then we will think of our commitment to Him in the sense of responding to His mercy, rather than fear of judgment, and hell fire. Look at the following verse, and consider that God's will for you is pleasing, and not burdensome to you.

Romans 12:1-2 (New Living Translation)

1 And so, dear brothers and sisters, I plead with you to give your bodies to God because of all he has done for you. Let them be a living and holy sacrifice—the kind he will find acceptable. This is truly the way to worship him.

2 Don't copy the behavior and customs of this world, but let God transform you into a new person by changing the way you think. Then you will learn to know God's will for you, which is good and pleasing and perfect.

The only way to not be conformed to this present world is to acknowledge our total and complete dependence upon Jesus, as far as our holiness, our peace, our inner strength, our joy, maturity, and depth of love. I am not a living sacrifice before God, by appearing to be more spiritual than others, by doing more church related activities than others, or by comparing myself to others.

2 Corinthians 10:12

12 For we dare not class ourselves or compare ourselves with those who commend themselves. But they, measuring themselves by themselves, and comparing themselves among themselves, are not wise.

If I am considering how righteous I am by my accomplishments, by my works, by my abilities, and by comparing those things to what others are doing, then I am deeply misguided. God finds none righteous, outside of those who are in Christ Jesus, and only pride will cause me to compare my righteousness to others. What I'm saying is that we must have relationship with Christ, through the searching of His Spirit within us, through intimacy with Him, relationship with Him, and longing to simply worship Him in spirit and in truth, in order to walk in genuine holiness, and righteousness. It is not of us, it is the gift of God. One good example of this is the story of Mary and Martha:

Luke 10:38-42

38 Now it happened as they went that He entered a certain village; and a certain woman named Martha welcomed Him into her house.

39 And she had a sister called Mary, who also sat at Jesus' feet and heard His word.

40 But Martha was distracted with much serving, and she approached Him and said, "Lord, do You not care that my sister has left me to serve alone? Therefore tell her to help me."

41 And Jesus answered and said to her, "Martha, Martha, you are worried and troubled about many things.

42 But one thing is needed, and Mary has chosen that good part, which will not be taken away from her."

Now, on the other side of the coin, we see the parable of the sheep and the goats, in Matthew 25:

Matthew 25:33-40

33 And He will set the sheep on His right hand, but the goats on the left.

34 Then the King will say to those on His right hand, 'Come, you blessed of My Father, inherit the kingdom prepared for you from the foundation of the world:

35 for I was hungry and you gave Me food; I was thirsty and you gave Me drink; I was a stranger and you took Me in;

36 I *was* naked and you clothed Me; I was sick and you visited Me; I was in prison and you came to Me.'

37 "Then the righteous will answer Him, saying, 'Lord, when did we see You hungry and feed *You,* or thirsty and give *You* drink?

38 When did we see You a stranger and take *You* in, or naked and clothe *You?*

39 Or when did we see You sick, or in prison, and come to You?'

40 And the King will answer and say to them, 'Assuredly, I say to you, inasmuch as you did *it* to one of the least of these My brethren, you did *it* to Me.'

When we read this parable, we come to understand that God is very concerned about what we actually do. Are our works good, or are they bad? "A tree is known by its fruit," Matthew 12:33. Two things to consider here; First of all, the righteous, according to the passage in Matt. 25, didn't seem to know that they had done anything special, as they said "when" did we do any of these things? It is apparent that the works that they did were a natural outflow of the love that was working within them. Secondly, as we consider a tree being known by its fruit, we can understand that a tree, in and of itself, has absolutely no ability to bear good fruit. In fact, the only possible thing that a fruit tree can do by itself, is to wither up and die, no matter how much it desires to bear the fruit that it was designed to bear. Now, if that tree is being soaked with nourishment, by watering, then that tree can bear good fruit. Only by soaking can the tree bear good fruit. It is the same with a believer in Christ. In scripture we are equated with branches. He is the vine, we are the branches.

John 15:5-6 (New Living Translation)

5 "Yes, I am the vine; you are the branches. Those who remain in me, and I in them, will produce much fruit. For apart from me you can do nothing.

6 Anyone who does not remain in me is thrown away like a useless branch and withers. Such branches are gathered into a pile to be burned.

We see in verse 6 that those branches that are unprofitable, unproductive, and unfruitful, which are to be cast into the fire to be burned, are branches that are simply not abiding in Jesus. So in retrospect, I am not a "good" branch, by doing good works, but by abiding in Jesus. The results of abiding in Him, are the works that are coming from us, that we are created in Christ Jesus to do. Outside of knowing Jesus intimately, all of my good works are in vain. Jesus' first priority with all of us is intimacy, relationship, and fellowship in the Spirit. On judgment day, Christ will have this to say to some:

Matthew 7:22-23

22 Many will say to Me in that day, 'Lord, Lord, have we not prophesied in Your name, cast out demons in Your name, and done many wonders in Your name?'

23 And then I will declare to them, 'I never knew you; depart from Me, you who practice lawlessness!'

As we see here, lawlessness is equated, biblically, with not knowing Jesus. How can we be so foolish as to do many works for Christ, and forsake the very thing that He desires of us in the first place? He longs to know us, and for us to know Him. Works are vital, but must only come as a result of knowing Christ in personal intimate relationship. Take a look at these verses in revelation:

Revelation 2:2-5 (New Living Translation)

2 "I know all the things you do. I have seen
your hard work and your patient endurance. I
know you don't tolerate evil people. You have
examined the claims of those who say they are
apostles but are not. You have discovered they
are liars.

3 You have patiently suffered for me without
quitting.

4 "But I have this complaint against you. You
don't love me or each other as you did at first!
5 Look how far you have fallen! Turn back to
me and do the works you did at first. If you
don't repent, I will come and remove your
lampstand from its place among the churches.

God says, "I know all about your good works,
and how you stand against evil. I see how you've
labored, and have not fainted in those labors, and
that's great, but I want your love. I want you!"
Many of us pray, "God use me, use me for your
glory." "Work through me, oh God." "I am your
vessel, oh God, please use me." What we must
see, is that God didn't create us to simply use us.
I've heard it said that we are not human doings,
but human beings. He created us for fellowship with Him. He goes on to say in Revelation
2, that they must repent. Repent of what? They
were doing nothing wrong, as far as works, but
He would not have their works without intimacy,
and he makes that abundantly clear as He says,
"Remember the love you used to have for me,

and have fallen away from. Repent of losing that love for me, and getting caught up in your righteous works as a way of pleasing me. Come back to the first work, the most important work that you will ever do. The work of walking in the fellowship of my affection and love, and if you do not, I will remove my oil. Your lamp will go out. You will be left with none of me."

Jesus spoke in John chapter 6 of eating His flesh, and drinking His blood, and as He did, He said that the words He spoke were "Spirit and they were life." He was talking of His desire for men to be consumed with Him, and not with what He could do for them, what sign He could provide for them, or in what they could do for Him. Hundreds were following Him at the time, and they were looking for a Messiah to come and overthrow the Romans. They were asking for another sign. He had already fed over 5,000 of them on the hillside, with a boy's lunch. Now they wanted more of Jesus' works on their behalf, but many of them had no interest in knowing Him. Many of them had no desire to see what He was attempting to teach them, that His kingdom does not come with observation, and that He desired for His kingdom to be revealed within them. God is love. Having that love revealed to us, and us returning that love to Him is God's greatest desire. He accomplishes that task through the working and moving of the Holy Spirit to us, and within us:

Luke 10:25-28 (New Living Translation) The Most Important Commandment

25 One day an expert in religious law stood up to test Jesus by asking him this question: "Teacher, what should I do to inherit eternal life?"

26 Jesus replied, "What does the law of Moses say? How do you read it?"

27 The man answered, "'You must love the Lord your God with all your heart, all your soul, all your strength, and all your mind.' And, 'Love your neighbor as yourself.'"

28 "Right!" Jesus told him. "Do this and you will live!"

Chapter 4

MEETING MY WIFE

In addition to ministry, our church was, well, just a fun church. We had hay rides, dinners on the grounds and trips to Six Flags. Famous singing groups, and well known evangelists came in on a regular basis. Christian contemporary rock groups came in to sing at the church, and during youth services. Many of these events were prime times to experience dating. By age 17 I was, unlike my friends, very interested in marriage. I wanted to be married, and looked forward to it. That being said, as I dated during those years, I was looking for characteristics, and qualities that I would like to have in a wife. What I mean by this is that I wasn't just looking to have fun on a date, chew bubble gum and make out. I wanted to talk about my future, her future, and where our lives were heading. I wanted to have serious conversations. There is an old song that says "she was too young to fall in love, and I was too young to know." I think this was partly what was going on with me, and a few girls I had dated. This led me to begin looking to date older girls. I had one date with an older, very spiritually mature young lady, named Robin. She picked me up, took me out for a steak, and paid the bill, at her request. She let it be known ahead of time, that she only desired friendship, and nothing more. While that was very nice, I still desired to be married.

Judy was a very special girl, about my age, and I liked her very much. She was serious, and committed to the Lord. Her mother would make me gooseberry pies, and her Dad took me fishing, but somehow we drifted apart, and although we had a very nice friendship, it seemed that it would not lead to marriage.

Kathy was 21, and I was 18, and we started dating. She was beautiful, and I fell head over heals for her. When we first began seeing each other on a regular basis, I was on cloud nine, as she would cling to my arm while I walked around in the church. The clinging of a beautiful young woman to the arm of a guy who felt the need for affirmation, seemed like heaven for a while, but suddenly, it seemed weird, and as though she needed affirmation much more than I. It seemed that she didn't feel that she could have her own identity, and that she felt the need to identify solely as my girlfriend. We had begun to discuss marriage, and the desire that we both had for that type of relationship, but the clinging was getting to me, and I knew that I needed to discuss this with her. One night, sitting in front of her apartment building in my car I told her all about my past, and asked if she would tell me of her past relationships, etc. She said, "Yes, I will tell you, if you promise that it will not make any difference in our relationship." I said, "Sure, nothing you could say would change my mind about how I feel about you." At that moment, she began sharing intimate details of a 2-year relationship that she had had with man that she had lived with, and who had kept her under tremendous bondage. Now I could begin to understand why she had such a lack of self-identity. Before she ever finished telling me the details, I knew that I would be breaking off my relationship with her that night. While this may sound cruel, to an 18 year old, who had never had sexual relations, it sounded like my worst nightmare, and I ended it tearfully that night. I didn't fully comprehend it at the time, but the Spirit of God was directing my steps. He is concerned about every area of our lives. God was directing Kathy's steps as well, and she later married a wonderful Christian man.

Betty Bruce was a troubled teen in our church, who had shot herself, had pulled a knife on one of our youth choir directors, and ended up in the psychiatric ward of a local hospital. I very much enjoyed encouraging people with life controlling issues, and so I went to visit her a few times. There was a pool table there, and we would talk while we played. As she got to know me she would say, "Tim, you have to meet my sister. Her name is Rebekah. I'm going to call her to come and visit." Many times, as Betty would mention Rebekah, I would reply with a polite, "Sure Betty, I'd love to meet her." All the while, keeping my thoughts on more important things to me at the moment, like the game of pool we were playing. Then it happened! It was around Halloween time, and we were having a fall festival at our church, in the school gym. The image is engraved upon my brain, as though it happened last week. Betty was walking towards me, with the most beautiful girl I had ever seen, and I thought, "Wow, who is that walking with Betty!" As they approached, Betty said, "Tim, I want you to meet my sister, Rebekah." "Hi," I said, as my heart began pumping faster by the second. She had long, magnificent brown hair, and was wearing a long brown winter coat. Our conversation was very brief, and that was it. Then on Sunday morning, while walking through the lobby of our church, there she was again. Our eyes met, and she waved at me. I was dumbfounded as to why this beautiful girl would be waving at me like that. This has always sounded strange to others that I've shared it with, but to me, it felt as though joy was enveloping every part of my soul, just to see this girl wave at me. All through service that morning, I couldn't stop thinking about her. After church that morning, we spoke, briefly, and exchanged addresses. The letters that we wrote each other over the next year are all in a safe place today. Through those letters, I discovered that this was the young lady that I desired greatly to marry.

Because my Dad still struggled somewhat with completely trusting me to be taking off out of town, especially to see a girl, I had to come up with inventive ways of dating Rebekah. Each and every one of our dates became a ministry engagement. I preached in her youth group, then to her cousins youth group. We passed out gospel tracks at a Mall in Alton, Illinois, etc. Phone bills were out of this world, which lead me to taking handfuls of change to the pay phone to talk as long as we could. I was working at Showbiz Pizza Place, and saving every dime. I decided to ask her to marry me. The most frightening aspect of this was to tell my Dad. You see, I was afraid of what he might think. What would he say? Surely he would never approve. I hadn't even told him that I liked Rebekah. When I finally told him that I planned to marry Rebekah, my Dad pulled out his wallet, handed me a credit card, and said, "You're going to need to purchase a ring."

Now, Rebekah and I had discussed marriage, but with the understanding that I couldn't afford a ring at that time, so needless to say, I was overjoyed with my Dad's gesture. I headed out to Kay's Jewelers, and bought a ring, which I presented to Rebekah at her house not long after. We were married 9 months after we met.

Before I go any further, I have to back up the story a little bit. You see, God's favor was with me. He was guiding my steps, even in revealing who He did not desire for me to marry. Before I ever met Rebekah, I had been accepted to attend CBC (Central Bible College). My Youth Pastor had already discussed the possibility of the church hiring me as an outreach Pastor upon graduation from Bible School. I was greatly looking forward to this potential ministry, and yet the Lord had other plans, and I was learning to hear His voice, and to recognize His distinctive direction in my life. One Sunday morning, my Parents had left for church and I was home alone, preparing to head to church. As I approached the front door, I began to sense the presence of the Lord in an unusual way. His presence was so strong that I could not bring myself to leave the house. For the next hour or so I lay on the floor, transfixed before the presence of the Lord. He spoke very clearly to me. In all honesty, this did not seem like a terribly unusual experience, because I was used to hearing from God in times of inter-cessions such as these. During that hour or so, the Lord spoke very definitely and clearly to me, as He said, "I do not desire for you to attend Bible School." When I heard that, my first thought was, "What will my Youth Pastor think?" Because the presence of the Lord was so powerful, and the word that He spoke to me so clear, I had no hesitation in my decision to back out of attending CBC. What I did not know was that, had I attended CBC, I would have never met Rebekah. I would have been long gone, before that wonderful day that she visited our church.

While my Youth Pastor was, and is, a mighty man of God, a man of great wisdom and discernment and a man who was greatly used of God for the shaping of my character in Christ, only God Himself can give a person specific details of certain life choices. Although we must also understand that we should make no major decisions without Godly counsel. I truly did follow the leading of the Spirit, as I simply allowed Him to search my heart that fateful day. While engaged to Rebekah, there were others who tried to discourage my plans to marry her. "You are too young." "You are messing up your life." "You don't know what you're doing." "We've never even seen her, or met her, and you're going to marry her?" The list of questions of my motives seemed endless, and yet, I'm quite certain they were questions that were coming out of genuine concern and love for me. This time of questioning helped me to determine whether I was hearing from God, or flesh. At our wedding, which took place in East Alton, Illinois, on July 2, 1983, there were quite a few friends that were not in attendance from my home church. Although this was very sad for me, the joy of following the will of the Lord for my life, was more fulfilling than I can express. I had been through much pain, much rejection, and much suffering in my short life, and now God was blessing me, and directing my steps. His favor was with me, and although I had no idea what would happen in the days to come, I was learning to walk by the leading of the Spirit of God. The day after we married, Rebekah and I moved to Houston Texas, as I sensed the Spirit of God was leading us there.

If you are not married, or have been divorced and desire to remarry, there is an understanding that can save you from heartache and divorce. That understanding is simply this – Don't use dating to find a spouse. Ask God to provide you with the one He has for you. The decision of marriage will be one of the most important decisions you'll make in this life. If you choose a spouse based on looks and emotional bonding, you are making a mistake. A person can fall in love with another person by emotional bonding at any time in their life. Before becoming emotionally bonded with another person, ask God for His will to be done. Let God direct your path in this area. This is one of the most difficult areas for many people to give to God because of our human, emotional desire for bonding. The problem of being driven by feelings and emotions is that the feelings and emotions can take on the voice of God. I've had people tell me on more than a few occasions that they knew they were to marry a certain person, and that God was telling them so. In reality, God was not involved in the process, but emotional bonding was controlling their decision-making. This type of emotional leading can be harmful to us in any major decision we're involved in, but it is especially harmful when you live by emotions in developing your relationships with other people. If you are going to be successful in living for God, you are going to do so by setting aside your emotional drive, and asking God for wisdom and discernment. A friend of mine said to me recently that "Dating is practice for divorce." I hadn't thought of that before, but there is truth in that statement. Let God's precious Holy Spirit fill you, and ask Him to direct you to the one He has for you to marry. If you are to marry, then God's plan involves the person that He has for you to marry, and He will provide. He did for me, and for many people I know. He will do it for you, as well.

Chapter 5

LIFE AND MINISTRY GROWTH

I was anxious for pulpit opportunities to help fulfill my calling, and to help develop my preaching ministry, and so we began attending a very small Assembly of God (A/G) church off of hwy 290. This church was small, but had an elderly Pastor, (H. A. Berry), who was a man with a great vision and ministry of helping young and upcoming ministers get going in the ministry. I had no idea at the time how he would impact my ministry and life, but was being led by the Spirit. Not long after beginning to attend this small church, brother Berry asked me to preach. I did, and then he asked again, and again. Pastor Berry had an illness in his voice box which prevented him from being able to speak clearly, and preaching had become extremely difficult for him. One day he walked into the TV store where I worked, handed me a bottle of anointing oil, and said "Please pray for me. I believe God to heal me." I was amazed at the confidence he had in me, and how he was taking me under his wing, and showing me the favor of God.

One day Pastor Berry called me and said, "There is a minister's fellowship meeting tonight, and you're going with me. I will be picking you up at 6:00." I said, "Yes, absolutely." Soon after, Pastor Berry was helping me to obtain the books and information I needed to begin my studies to obtain my ministerial credentials. I followed through, as I studied at home through the Assemblies of God approved program through Berean College. Pastor Berry sat on the committee who approved me for credentialing, as I obtained my "Christian Workers Papers." I would later complete enough Bible Schooling through Berean, now a University, to obtain my license to preach, and be qualified for ordination with the Assemblies of God. Again God's Spirit was leading. When you walk in the Spirit, by spending time waiting in His presence daily and seeking to know Him more intimately, what you are doing is giving Him access to your soul. You open the door, and allow Him to lead you and direct your steps.

After receiving my Christian Workers Papers (ordination documentation), I was now able to secure employment as a minister in an A/G church, and so began pursuing my calling in that regard. My brother in law had left "Giant Screen

TV" and a new manager was hired at Giant Screen. My brother in law, Gary, was and is the most convincing salesman I've ever known. When he left Giant Screen, sales went down, way down! I was suddenly moved from salary plus commission to commission only. My calling was preaching, not selling TV's and the Lord was letting me know that it was time to press into my calling. In the meantime, Rebekah was working long hours at a finance company. Rebekah always desired to do an above average job in whatever she did, and this job was no exception. Attending church, even midweek services was not only important to me, but it was not something I was willing to miss for any reason, especially not for Rebekah's overtime hours. We had one vehicle, and I would go in to pick her up, and her boss would say something like, "Oh, the girls didn't get their work done, and must stay late to finish." At the same time I found out that these girls were working off the clock, as they were told to clock out at 5:00 and continue working. I confronted Rebekah's boss, and he wouldn't give in. Rebekah had such a drive to please those that she worked for that she wouldn't dream of complaining. One day, upon arriving home, I confronted Rebekah, and told her that it was wrong, that I didn't want her working late, and that I didn't want to miss Wednesday night services. Rebekah suddenly froze up. She became completely unresponsive. More concerning to me than this was that I could sense an attack of the enemy against her, and if Satan was coming against her, then he was coming against me, against our unity, and against our relationship. I tried repeatedly to get her to open up to me, and to the Lord through prayer, but nothing was working. Oppression had filled our apartment. Rebekah had felt, many times, as though she couldn't measure up spirituality to me or to other Christians. She felt at times, as though I could touch God, but that she couldn't. This was nothing more than oppressiveness, but at the time I had little idea of how to handle it. I was upset with Rebekah. "How could she not speak to me?" "Why in the world would she act like this?" I'd like for you to understand that walking in the Spirit, being led by the Spirit, and even helping others who are in need of victory, is not something that is reserved only for experienced, seasoned ministers, and/or, Christian counselors and psychologists. I didn't even know exactly what it was that I was up against, but I did recognize, very quickly, that it was a spiritual battle. That I was not wrestling with flesh and blood. My enemy was not my wife, but Satan, who is the father of lies. This father of lies was lying to Rebekah. The same desires that she had felt most of her life, concerning going the extra mile to please people, was now affecting her fellowship with God. "I'm not spiritual," she thought. I remember reading of how Paul, the apostle felt this way in Romans chapter 7, and how he came to the understanding that Jesus was the only righteous one, and the one who would rescue him.

That night, as Rebekah battled these thoughts and emotions, I went into our bedroom as she sat there motionless, and lifelessly on the couch. I began to cry out to God on her behalf. I began to intercede, and as I did, I began to sense the boldness of the Holy Spirit. I went back into the living room, where Rebekah was, and began speaking love over her. "You are loved of God, Rebekah!" "You are His child, and nothing can change that!" I began to weep, as the presence of God increased in the room. "You are free, Rebekah!" I continued, "You are free from all condemnation." I spoke many things over her that night, as the heaviness lifted and the love of God filled the room, and the joy of the Lord filled Rebekah.

It turned out that the expectations that Rebekah's boss was placing on her, and on the other girls working there, were illegal expectations. Her boss was fired, not long after.

Having Jesus, and now Rebekah in my life was like being given a new lease on life. Every day, in spite of the daily struggles of a young married couple, was filled with joy and anticipation of new things. Speaking of new things, we discovered that Rebekah was "with child," and we were overjoyed. We were both making good money, and Rebekah had pregnancy coverage with her employer. Five months into the pregnancy something went wrong. I was at work when I received a call from the hospital with the words, "Mr. Wiebe, we need for you to get to the hospital right away." I asked what was wrong, but they wouldn't say. I darted from the TV store, and raced to the hospital to find that the baby had died in the womb, and immediate action was required. Labor was induced, and, after several hours of labor, Rebekah delivered our first child. There is such anguish at a time such as this that you have thoughts of "Why God?" "Why would you do this to us?" "Why would you allow this to happen to our baby?" "What have we done to deserve this?" "Will we ever be able to have a healthy baby?" The love and comfort of friends and family could not replenish the loss of the child, but God was there. We may have had a moment of losing sight of Him, but God was right there in our midst, loving us, strengthening us, and comforting us. When life deals such blows to us as believers, how are we to handle it? Should we believe that we were just not close enough to the Lord? That we were being punished for not being as holy and good as we should have been? We can lose out on the blessings of God, simply by not trusting Him when we don't understand why something has happened. While God will allow our faith to be tested, He will never leave us and never forsake us. We may never know, in this lifetime, why some terrible things happen to us, but we must not let go of the truth that is in Jesus. God loves you deeply. He has a plan for the success and blessing of your future. What you and I must do is to trust Him. Trusting God does not allow us to let go of His promises, or to forsake Him when something goes horribly wrong in the natural.

Trusting God means that I am not going to trust what I understand about a situation. Whatever happens in this life is temporal. Scripture tells us that we are aliens, and strangers, and that we are not of this world. If we live, live for Christ. If we die, it's only gain. Do I know that God is working all things for my benefit? The answer is abundantly, YES!

Proverbs 3:3-6 (New Living Translation)

3 Never let loyalty and kindness leave you!
Tie them around your neck as a reminder.
Write them deep within your heart.
4 Then you will find favor with both God and people, and you will earn a good reputation.
5 Trust in the LORD with all your heart;
do not depend on your own understanding.
6 Seek his will in all you do,
and he will show you which path to take.

Chapter 6

FULL TIME MINISTRY

Rebekah and I went into full time ministry in Alvin, Texas as youth ministers, and working in a Christian school. This lasted about a year and a half. Our son Timmy was born during that time. From there, the Lord directed our steps to Humble Texas, where I was an Assistant Pastor, and then on to a position as Senior Pastor In Stamford, TX, from there to full time evangelism, and from there to Merkel, TX, where we Pastored 11 years. We are currently Pastoring our third church, located in Georgetown, TX. In the past 24 years of ministry, we have faced many attacks as Satan came against us. We have faced verbal abuse from people, as well as the attacks of Satan in areas of our flesh and fleshly weaknesses. Brokenness before God has brought us through all of that, and brokenness is what will sustain us in Christ. At times when I have felt mistreated by others, I can feel the natural instinct to become bitter.

Becoming bitter and resentful is a natural result of certain events taking place similar to what I'm describing, but natural results are not what God is after. He is after supernatural results within us. He is interested in us laying down our pride. Our pride that says, "I don't deserve this!" "I'm a man of god, and I'll not subject myself to being treated like this."

Those were all thoughts and many more that have all gone through my head. "I'll never subject myself to the possibility of this kind of pain again," I've thought. The trouble with this is that Jesus subjected Himself to much worse. He allowed the religious leaders to hate Him, to persecute Him, to denounce Him, and to crucify Him. He gave up all of His rights willingly, and He was God incarnate. Who was I? Was I more deserving than Christ, of being treated with respect? It is only by humility that we come to a place of greatness in the sight of God. Paul said "I am crucified with Christ, and I no longer live..." Was I to put myself above Paul or even above Christ? Giving up all of our rights, as it relates to our pride, is the way to God's blessing in our lives. It is the way that we find the path of His perfect direction. As long as I don't allow myself to be hurt by people, I'll not go far in God's kingdom. Jesus said, "If they hated me, they will hate you also." Persecution generally comes as a result of the world's reaction to the anointing of the Spirit of God on ones life. Do I want to walk in that anointing, or is it more important for me to be respected by men, as I demand to be respected? Many people, who have been called of God into ministry, have let go of that calling because of the fear of man.

Man didn't call me, or you, and man cannot keep us from the ministry that God has called us to. Only I can do that, by allowing hurt to fester, and to cause me to fear pursuing ministry positions that make me vulnerable to those potential hurts.

After about a year and a half at Stamford, and after facing a few fires of the church politic variety, I was determined to stay as long as God would have us there in Stamford. We were not at all unhappy, and the church was being blessed. One day though, as Rebekah and I were rehearsing a song to sing at church, the Lord spoke to me. In the song were the words, "if you could see where Jesus brought me from, to where I am today, then you would know the reason why I love Him so." Each time as we would get to this part of the song, I was not able to sing, as I was fighting back the tears, and realizing that the Lord was dealing with my heart. Rebekah would back up the accompaniment tape, and again I couldn't get past that part of the song, so I said, "Honey, I have to spend some time in prayer." At that moment, I went to the bedroom of the Parsonage, and cried out to God. "What is it, Lord? What are you desiring of me?" He spoke clearly and precisely to me as the Holy Spirit said, "I want you to take the message I've put in your heart. I want you to take it to the churches." I said, "Yes Lord," and we immediately began to make arrangements to go out on the evangelistic field, full time. We put in two weeks notice at the church, sold all of our furniture, purchased a travel trailer, and began sleeping in it, parked in front of the church Parsonage, as all of our furniture was now gone.

Traveling Full Time

Being an evangelist, and living in a travel trailer with our 2 children was both exciting and challenging. A new type of faith was necessary, a faith to just go and trust that God would open the doors, and lead the way. A faith that would not lean to my understanding of things, and that would say, "I'll go where you say to go Lord, and trust you completely for meeting our financial needs." I had put out letters to hundreds of churches in the state of Texas, and a few calls were coming in. The very first message I received regarding holding a revival was from an elderly Pastor in San Angelo, Texas, Pastor Cecil Vaughn. Pastor Vaughn and his wife had dedicated most of their lives completely to the ministry of the gospel of Christ. They had been Pastor to many churches, and had been pastoring East Angelo Assembly of God for about 30 years. As I listened to the message they had left on my answering machine, it went something like this, "Brother Wiebe, I received your letter, have prayed over it, and feel that the Lord would have me to invite you to preach a revival meeting for us here. I have to tell you, though, that we have only a handful of people at this time, and most of them are elderly women, on a fixed income. We desire for you to come, but I can't promise much in the way of an offering." I listened to that message and thought, "Ok, we will go there, but first I need to schedule a meeting or two in larger churches, where we have enough offering money to sustain us for a while." As I thought on that, the Spirit of God said, "No, go to San Angelo first." I had learned to hear and know His voice, and I knew He was leading the way, so I called brother Vaughn and scheduled the revival meeting. Brother Vaughn informed me that they had evangelist quarters inside the church, and so we left our trailer, and went. Looking back now, sleeping in an old dusty church building may not have been the greatest of ideas, especially since we had a travel trailer, but we will never forget those types of experiences. On the first Sunday morning of this week long revival, we were in for a pleasant surprise. We had done what God had asked us to do. We were willing to follow the leading of His Spirit and now we were witness to a great blessing. Pastor Vaughn, without our knowledge, had decided to retire. There was a new Pastor there, whom Pastor Vaughn was grooming to replace him, and there were more people there than usual (about 70 total) that Sunday morning. Many were saved, filled with the Spirit of God, and blessed by His presence. It was a glorious day, and a glorious revival meeting. The offering given to us that week was over a thousand dollars. God will take care of us, as we set aside our own understanding, our own agenda, and follow His lead, and His will.

For the next year and a half we traveled, singing and preaching in churches over the state of Texas, and some in Oklahoma, living with our two boys in our travel trailer. One Pastor, from south Texas called, saying, "Brother Timothy, I received your letter, requesting a service with us, and I threw it away. I threw it away three times, and just could not let it go." He said, "In over 25 years of ministry, I've never had anyone to preach for me who I didn't personally know, but the Holy Spirit will not leave me alone about your letter." This Pastor requested that we come for a Sunday service in order to decide if he desired to have us for a weeklong revival meeting, or not. We came for a Sunday. God blessed the service, and he scheduled us for a revival. During that revival meeting there were 8 young people called into full time ministry, along with salvations, and baptisms in the Holy Spirit.

Testing's and Trials.... Again

Rebekah, now pregnant with our daughter Rachel, was struggling somewhat to keep up with our traveling schedule. Thanksgiving and Christmas time was nearing, and scheduling revival meetings was not the top priority of most of the Pastors that I knew. And contacting them for services was producing nothing but an empty and blank calendar for us. Suddenly I found that we had nothing scheduled for the next couple of months or so. We were walking by faith, or at least were attempting to, and yet our only source of income was derived from my preaching ministry. With no meetings scheduled, there was no money left and none coming in. We had a travel trailer payment, food to buy, 2 kids to provide for and one more on the way, and our money was gone. Looking back now, I feel that I should have continued to travel to various churches, just believing God to open the opportunities for ministry, while keeping ourselves in that place of complete dependence on the leading of the Spirit of God. Instead I took a job as a security guard, and went to work guarding a hotel-parking garage in downtown Houston. We had parked our trailer at my mother-in-law's house in New Caney, Texas, and my mission-vision began to slip. Discouragement began to set in, as I worked 8 hour outdoor shifts, guarding parked cars in one of the coldest Houston winters that I can remember. For the next couple of months I went up and down those 10 floors, wondering where my life was heading. What was I doing? Why were there no ministry opportunities? Pneumonia had settled into my lungs, but I had to keep working. Should I seek to pastor a church again? Several of the churches that we had ministered in, were shepherded by elderly Pastors who had brought us in, specifically with the hope that we would run with their vision and take over as Pastor of their church. Although it was flattering to have those desires disclosed to us, we sensed no leading of the Lord in that direction, and were very happy to be doing what we were doing in our ministry. Now there was no ministry, and just attending church became difficult for me. I found that allowing thoughts of discouragement to fester is a quick way to lose your focus. Other thoughts can begin to move in when discouragement is unresolved. I began to battle thoughts of envy of other ministers, and possibly some bitterness as well.

In the garage where I was working, the hotel manager would come out to smoke a cigarette, and would talk with me as he did. I was so discouraged, felt so defeated, that I had no desire to tell him that

I was a preacher. And so I didn't. Our conversations were shallow, and revolved around sports, or the weather. One day, as he stood there smoking his cigarette, he looked intently at me and said something completely shocking and amazing to me. He said, "You are a preacher aren't you." "Yes," I said, in disbelief. I hadn't told anyone. We worked in shifts, where only one security officer worked in the garage at a time. My interaction with the other officers and other people in general, was almost completely non-existent, and I had not mentioned to anyone that I was a minister. This was a lonely job, where just staying awake was a major battle at times. There was no one to talk to besides this hotel manager. I replied, "How did you know?" He said, "I know because the Lord revealed it to me." "I am a backslidden preacher," he continued. "I left the ministry long ago, taking this job, and forsaking my calling," he said. Tears began to well up in his eyes as he said, "Don't you forsake your calling." "You know this is a dead end job for you. You're not supposed to be here." We talked a while, my shift ended, and I went home. Now, God was stirring my heart again. He hadn't left me alone. He hadn't forgotten about us, and he used a backslidden preacher to speak to me. I went home, and that same day scheduled 9 revivals back to back. I quit that job, and we began traveling once again.

Now we were traveling with 3 children, as our daughter had been born in Houston. Souls were being saved, and people were being impacted by the love and power of God as we traveled from church to church. We had no cell phone, and my Mom and Dad received our mail, and phone messages. Though not easy, this was an extremely blessed time of our lives. Between revivals, we would park our RV at a State Park, or KOA Camp, and enjoy a few days relaxing with the kids.

The many experiences that we had were helping to shape us, helping to give us experience in working with people, with all of their troubles and trials, as well as to see the many struggles that Pastors were facing. People need love. They need God. What they didn't need was just another sermon. Church going people have heard sermons all their lives, and they've heard plenty of good gospel music. I wanted to see God move in each and every service where we ministered. I was not, could not, be content with simply having a schedule, and singing, preaching, and picking up a paycheck at the end of the week. I genuinely wanted to see lives impacted by the Spirit of God. Prayer was vital. Intercession for each service was vital. "Help these people, oh God. Pour out your Spirit upon them. Do what you want to do. Help me to get out of the way." This was my constant prayer. I had absolutely no interest in "big" ministry, making a name for myself, or becoming a well-known evangelist. It never crossed my mind, really. I was consumed with love for God, and love for people. I wanted to see captives being set free, and we were seeing this happen. I had no desire to come off the evangelistic field, but traveling with three young children was becoming more difficult, especially as the boys began to approach school age.

Chapter 7

11 YEARS IN MERKEL, TEXAS

A s I contemplated these things, it seems that the Lord was directing us to settle down, and to pastor a church again. I had preached a couple of revival meetings at Merkel, which is located between Sweetwater, and Abilene, on Interstate 20. They were meeting in an unfinished brick building, with no roof over the sanctuary. They met in the fellowship hall for services, which only had a concrete floor, and a makeshift platform. This was the only room in this 10,000 square foot building with painted walls. The people had been moved out of the old facility, which had been build in the 1940's, and had been moved into the unfinished building by a previous Pastor, who had a good vision, and had hopes of seeing the building completed after moving in. People became discouraged though, at the slow process and some had left the church. There were about 20 people in attendance when we had held a couple of revivals there. I could see that this building and location had great potential, and in the old building they had once been running around 200 in regular attendance. But I was no builder, and the Pastor there at the time was a builder, as were the previous 2 Pastors before him. In the meantime, we still had several revivals scheduled, and one of those was to be in a small town about an hour south of San Angelo, Texas. I was excited about ministry in this church, because I had heard reports of a great move of God there, and that the church had boomed suddenly in growth from about 50 to 140 people. In preparation for this scheduled revival, I gave a quick call to the Pastor, who immediately informed me of his decision to resign his Pastorate, and that he would have to cancel the revival meeting. He told me of how blessed the church was, and that his decision was not based on any church trouble, but that he felt that the Lord wanted to move him elsewhere. He said that he would be resigning on the following Sunday, and with that in mind, I thought I'd be the first to contact the local Presbyter, regarding the potential of coming to Pastor this church. As I called the Presbyter, making this request, he said without hesitation, "Oh, that church already has a new Pastor." I felt my heart sink, as I heard those words. "How can they have a new Pastor, since the current Pastor hasn't even left yet?" "A good friend of the Pastor there, (Terry Allen), is taking over as their new Pastor," he said. Terry Allen was the Pastor of the church at Merkel. "Why don't you consider coming to Pastor the Merkel church?" It took me all of about 2 seconds, or less, to say "No, I'm not really interested in going there, but thanks for offering." I quickly got off the phone, and didn't have another thought about pastoring the church, (First Assembly of God) at Merkel. On the following day, as I walked through the living room of my parent's house in Cypress, Texas, praying, the Spirit of the Lord again began to speak to my heart. "I want you to go to Merkel," He said. I've made many mistakes over the years, but one thing that has kept me, protected me, and blessed my life immensely, is that I have learned to hear the voice of the Spirit of God, and have been willing to heed His voice, knowing that He has the best plans for me, and my family. I called Presbyter Stone that same day, and asked how soon I could come to minister at Merkel. He said, "How about this coming Sunday," and I said, "That sounds great!" That Sunday was the first Sunday in August, 1992, and became my first Sunday of 11 years of at Merkel Texas.

It was the Best and Worst of Times

Merkel was a place of hopes, dreams, aspirations and expectations for us. As we started out there, there were very little funds, a handful of members, a building that was less than half finished, and I was, at first not able to draw a salary. Because of this, I found employment as a school bus driver. I really enjoyed driving a bus, it was not bad pay for only a couple of hours a day, and I drove for the next 7 years.

There was a woman attending the church, who had started coming when we came there. Her name was Suzanne. Rebekah and I had not gotten to know this woman yet, and one day after service, while shaking her hand, she said these words, "I'm not as bad as you think I am." What a strange statement. We had not had any bad feelings about her. All we knew of her was that she was attending, and that she seemed a little shy, and timid. There was an obvious struggle within her, and we would soon be finding out some of the depths of that struggle.

People can become extremely comfortable in holding onto a stronghold of hurt and bitterness. Deep down they know they need to be free, and even may desire freedom, but now they are feeling threatened in the sense that victory requires a humbling, as well as a complete change of thought, as it regards their upbringing and what they've been taught about God. There is no liberty in Christ Jesus for a person, without humility and a change of thinking. Repentance is a change, not only of action, but of thought. It is a place of humility before God, as well as trusting in His mercy and grace. Humility is more than an outward look. It is first, an inward change of heart and thought.

Luke 18:10-14 (New Living Translation)
10 "Two men went to the Temple to pray. One was a Pharisee, and the other was a despised tax collector.

11 The Pharisee stood by himself and prayed this prayer: 'I thank you, God, that I am not a sinner like everyone else. For I don't cheat, I don't sin, and I don't commit adultery. I'm certainly not like that tax collector!

12 I fast twice a week, and I give you a tenth of my income.'

13 "But the tax collector stood at a distance and dared not even lift his eyes to heaven as he prayed. Instead, he beat his chest in sorrow, saying, 'O God, be merciful to me, for I am a sinner.' 14 I tell you, this sinner, not the Pharisee, returned home justified before God. For those who exalt themselves will be humbled, and those who humble themselves will be exalted."

Those who worked with Suzanne (fellow employees), knew her as a friendly, outgoing person who smiled and laughed a lot. It would be some time before Rebekah and I would come to know the real Suzanne, the Suzanne that God knew was there, the Suzanne who would come to understand forgiveness, inner healing, peace, joy, happiness, contentment, and deliverance from the fear and bitterness of the past. I remember having many God given thoughts, and visions of the Lord's desires for Suzanne. One time, while in prayer, I began to have an intense burden for her, and I saw in vision a beautiful flower unfolding, and opening up. I felt God's love for Suzanne, and His desire to bring her to a place of blossoming, like that flower. There were so many beautiful gifts locked up inside of her. She was a precious person with a tremendous amount of compassion for hurting people, but we were not yet witnessing this because of the hurt that she herself had locked up inside. There is an old saying that says, "Hurting people hurt people." Suzanne was hurting, and she was allowing that hurt to cause a root of bitterness within her.

The thing that Rebekah and I had to learn was to understand was that the Lord had placed this person into our lives. I had much to learn in the way of spiritual warfare. Pastor Countryman, from Humble, used to have a saying that he picked up somewhere, that said, "People need loving the most, when they deserve it the least." Many times, when a person is an agitation to you, and that agitation is purposeful, it will give you (in the natural understanding), anything but loving thoughts toward that person. As believers in Christ, we must learn to be a people of the Spirit, a people who are learning to walk in the Spirit, and to live by the Spirit of God in ever increasing measure. The love of Christ, flowing through us, by His Spirit, is the only way that we are truly going to have an impact for God in the lives of those whom God places in our lives.

Suzanne was in a soulish battle, a confrontation between things seen and things eternal. This battle, within her, was causing a problem in relation to spiritual authority, and particularly, the authority that Rebekah and I, as her Pastors, represented. There were times when I would be preaching, and I would suddenly sense a quenching of the Spirit of God. There was a very distinctive and definite oppression of the enemy that was with Suzanne. One of the problems with this type of oppression is that it will not only affect the person afflicted with it, but at times will also have an impact on others, especially family members and other church members. I couldn't prove it, and there was no definite or obvious thing that I could point out at the time, but I knew that there was a quenching of the Spirit in the church. I also knew that it was an oppression that was hovering over Suzanne. This was not something that I was going to be able to battle, or take care of with my own strength, or with my natural understanding of things. Besides this, there were actually times that Suzanne acknowledged to us that she was aware of the oppression, and that she felt responsible for quenching the Spirit in the church. The enemy desired to keep us from revival, and to keep Suzanne, and anyone else that he could, in a state of bondage to past hurts, bitterness, resentment, and an overall lack of holy authority in their lives.

I believe very strongly in being transparent. Scripture is clear that we are not to put on a facade. We are not to be phonies. As a Pastor, or leader, we must allow people to see who we really are. That we are in ministry to reflect Christ and His goodness, rather than to show how "wonderful" we are, or how great "our ministry" is. I may be a Pastor, but I am also human. I am as imperfect as they come, and the worst sinner that we can imagine who comes to Christ, is every bit as good as me, or anyone else for that matter. We are not good and holy by virtue of holding a position in the church, or by an outward appearance of righteousness, and that needs to be understood by the congregation. It is Christ who keeps my heart healed and whole. I know and recognize that there is nothing good within my own heart, except for surrender to the Spirit and will of God. He alone is able to make us (and keep us) whole and capable of ministry in His Spirit.

In the position that I have as Pastor, there is an anointing. This anointing is given by God for service, for edification, for bringing healing and blessing in the church, to people's lives. This anointing must not be abused, by having an attitude that says - "Look at me, I'm anointed." I've seen preachers abuse the anointing of God on their lives, in making statements similar to this - "You people just don't get it, and you're never going to get it. God has revealed deep, deep secrets to me, that you could never know, and I'm trying to teach you, but maybe I'm wasting my time. Don't you see that I have received revelation?" When preachers say things like this, they hold their position and particular anointing in high regard, rather than putting the emphasis on what God regards highly, — PEOPLE!

God loves people. He loves them when they mess up. He loves them when they hurt, when they hurt themselves, and when they hurt others. As a preacher of the Word of God, pointing people to my goodness is pointless and a waste of everyone's time. It is an abuse of position and my anointing. My ultimate goal in fulfilling my calling must be to help people come to see who they are in Christ, and what Christ is doing and desires to do in their lives. My goal must not ever be to make a name for myself because of the "revelations" I've received from the Lord. Any revelation I receive from the Spirit of God is for the purpose of blessing people, and helping them to see Christ, and not me. In scripture, Paul said:

2Co 11:29 Who is weak, and I am not weak? Who is caused to stumble, and I do not burn?
2Co 11:30 If it is right to boast, I will boast *of* the things of my weakness. (MKJV)

Why is it that as a preacher, so many find it necessary to appear so unblemished. We are all needy people. If I am to minister the grace, love and freedom of God, I must demonstrate that I am continually experiencing His presence and power in my own life, and that I have need of experiencing His grace daily.

2Co 12:9 And He said to me, My grace is sufficient for you, for My power is made perfect in weakness. Most gladly therefore I will rather glory in my weaknesses, that the power of Christ may overshadow me.

2Co 12:10 Therefore I am pleased in weaknesses, in insults, in necessities, in persecutions, in distresses for Christ's sake; for when I am weak, then I am powerful. (MKJV)

I believe that Suzanne witnessed the anointing of God working in me and Rebekah as we preached, and lead worship. I also believe that she looked at herself in light of that anointing, and thought—"They must really think I'm unholy." I believe that God, by His Spirit, was searching Suzanne's heart. He was drawing her to freedom and to victory, and he was using me in my gifting and calling as a Pastor to help to draw her to that freedom. I believe that her thoughts of unworthiness, and thoughts of ungodliness were simply thoughts of condemnation brought on her by Satan, as the Lord attempted to bring her to healing and victory. When a person doesn't understand or accept the free gift of God's grace, they will inevitably begin to attempt to justify themselves, and to compare their goodness with others. Now there we were, not really knowing anything about Suzanne, and as we shake her hand, she says, "I'm not as bad as you think I am." It hurt to hear those words, because it seemed like a personal affront. "What makes her think that we think she's bad?" "How in the world did she ever get that impression?" This statement hurt because I thought of myself as a man of love, a man of compassion who truly and genuinely cared about people. Looking back now, I can see that she was simply resisting the work of the Spirit of God in her life, and not trusting that God was going to do a good work in her. She was more than likely, in essence, saying these words to the God who's anointing was speaking to her. In essence she was saying, "God, I know that you see me. I know that you know all about me and that you are drawing me to you, but I'm okay. I'll be alright, just leave me alone, I'm just not as bad as you think I am."

Suzanne's husband, at that time, did not attend church. They had two daughters, and we soon become friends with them. Although her husband did not attend church, he and I became friends. Rebekah and I, along with our young children, would go over to their house in the evenings, and go for long walks with them, talking, sharing, and getting to know each other. They had a trampoline, and since I still considered myself a recycled teenager, I would jump on with our boys, and their girls. During the coming weeks and months we got close to this family. Whether we were at their house, our house, or at a State Park, we always had a good time with them. Her husband William and I would play basketball together, and even joined a city league in Abilene. Our relationship with this family, for the most part, was joyful and peaceful, on a non-spiritual relationship level.

Being Suzanne's Pastor, and representing a spiritual influence, was not at all peaceful for many years, however. Again, I believe the reasons behind this have much to do with her struggle to let go of things that God was trying to deal with in her life. The Lord greatly desired to move in her life in a beautiful and holy way, and to a great degree she was resisting this. Since Rebekah and I were leading the church spiritually, and attempting to lead people to freedom and victory in Christ, it stands to reason that Suzanne would have negative feelings towards us. If God Himself is misunderstood, and is seen as a threat to some Christians, (according to their understanding), then those whom God places in that person's life may also indeed be misunderstood and seen as a threat. We were loving the people of the church, loving Suzanne, and her family, but I believe her thoughts may have been along the lines of, "They don't think I'm good enough for them." or "They want me to change." etc. I am still in the lifelong process, myself, of learning how wonderful, awesome, beautiful, and glorious the work of God is in our lives. He loves us so much, and when He changes us, it is He who does the good work. We yield ourselves, submit, and surrender to His work, but the work of grace, is His work alone. Suzanne ultimately came to understand this, and today is walking in the fulfillment of the call, and plan of God for her life. Suzanne walks today in the understanding of the deep love of God. Although Suzanne had been baptized previously, I had the privilege of baptizing her in water again, as she recognized publicly the work of love that God had done within her. I also had the privilege of performing the wedding ceremony for their oldest daughter a few years ago. I asked Suzanne if she would share, in her own words, the work of God in her life. Here, below, is her testimony, in her own words. Praise God for His faithful and uncondi-tional love.

"Satan started early in my life setting up mental strongholds and trying to destroy the good plan God had for me. He actually began before I was ever conceived. My parents were separated and heading for a divorce. My mother went to visit my father and I was conceived as a result of their visit. They got back together but their marriage did not last. I believe their separation before I was born was Satan's first attempt at my life. I was raised the youngest daughter of five girls by a single mom. My mother worked hard and did the best she could with the circum-stances she faced. We went to church most of the time and I learned a lot about God. The things we were taught (or at least the way I perceived them) seemed impossible for a young girl to follow. Things like be good, don't sin, girls can't wear makeup or pants and couldn't cut their hair, etc. My environ-ment was very legalistic and I was never taught about God's love for me, nor that He was full of grace and mercy. My life was a list of rules and I could never seem to measure up. This feeling of never being able to do everything right was a source of great discour-agement to me. In my child-like thinking I truly believed if I sinned it was over. There was no hope left. I always wanted to please and serve God, but would give up trying, thinking I couldn't, that some how I was different because others seemed to be able to live a Christian life and I couldn't. These feelings combined with emotional, mental, physical and sexual abuse took a real toll on my personality. I became shy, introverted and insecure. It would only be later in my life and after much work of the Holy Spirit that I came to realize I was not shy at all. I always felt like an outsider. I realize now that Satan planted all of those feelings and thoughts in my mind but as a young child I never saw his scheme. At the age of eleven, Satan would take his second attempt at my life. I almost drowned in a lake, at an unsupervised outing. A young man I did not know, rescued me from water above my head and an under current I couldn't swim against. Satan thought he had me but God had other plans. As I became older I began to think all the more that it was impossible for me to serve God. As a teenager I was pretty typical. I still attended church but only because I had to. I still had a strong desire to please God and had repented of my sins many times. And though I had tried and tried, I just did not understand how to live a life pleasing to God or that God was interested in me and wanted an intimate relationship with me. I was so bound that I didn't even know how to receive God's love and actually became fearful of Him. This fear of God and feelings of failure to serve Him led me to a life of running from God. A life filled with despair, discouragement, depression, anger, bitterness and no hope. In my young adult years I found myself married with two young children. With the responsibility of motherhood came the constant concern of where my children would spend their eternity. God wasn't spoken about much in our home but I knew my children needed Him. I believe the Holy Spirit put my deep concern for my children in my heart. I became so concerned that I began to search out a church to attend. Somehow I just knew my children could serve God even though I didn't think I could and I felt it was up to me to make sure they would be taught God's word and be faithful to His house. After many years and much searching, God led me to Abundant Life Church. God provided us with a wonderful pastor and his wife who would teach us much about God's word and His love, not only in word but also in deed. What I didn't know at the time was that God had lead me to this church not only for my children but to do an awesome work in my own heart and life, a work that only He can do. At Abundant Life Church I began to be taught God's word in a way I had never heard before. It was confusing to me at first, because I had never heard much about God's love, grace and mercy and there didn't seem to be too many rules to follow. But at the same time it was something I greatly desired. I was being taught how to live a Christian life and have a relationship with Jesus instead of just trying to follow a bunch of rules and fearing if I messed up that God would be angry with me and no longer accept me. Even though I was learning much about God's love, grace and mercy, I didn't know how to apply it to my life which caused even more confusion, frustration and again feelings and thoughts that I just didn't have what it takes. No one really understood how I felt. It was a time of constant emotional highs and lows and most of the relationships in my life became very strained. I knew what I was being taught was the truth but I just couldn't understand why it didn't seem to work for me. There was great condemnation and I knew I was born again, but my actions were not matching my confession. Some even thought I was demon possessed. I knew demon possession was impossible for a believer but Satan was in control of my thoughts, actions and emotions. After living like this for several years and not understanding the importance of having my mind constantly renewed with the word of God, I sank into a great depression, a depression so great I was just existing, unable to get out of bed and function a lot of days. I wanted to be free but freedom seemed impossible. Thank God all things are possible with Him. Even though some people gave up on me, God never gave up and I know he has promised to complete the good work He has begun in me. He saw my heart when others only saw my actions. I didn't realize that all the negative, condemning thoughts that Satan placed in my mind were not my thoughts. Wrong thought patterns had always been a part of me and I believed that was just the way I was: thoughts of negativity, hurt, shame, depression etc. Some how I always managed to come out of any low state of depression when it was time to go to church again. Even though in my natural mind I didn't feel like I fit in with other believer's, I still found a drawing so strong that I always managed to make it to the next service. I had such a longing for God's touch that I was in church just about every time the doors were open. All I knew was that deep down I had a love for God and longed to know him more and to please Him. I am very grateful for a pastor who consistently preached the truth because it was the truth of God's word that would set me free. It was only after I began to just believe what the Word said and that it was for me and to submit and yield to the Holy Spirit, and allow Him to search me, that God began a radical transformation in my life. I love being in God's presence. It is in His presence that we are truly changed. It took years for me to learn to relax in the presence of the Lord. But once I learned, things in my life began to change at a rapid rate. The more I heard the word, believed it and applied it to my life the more I began to change. As a result of seeking Him, Jesus baptized me in the Holy Spirit with the evidence of speaking in tongues. What a glorious gift God has provided us, where we can fellowship with Him in the Spirit and be edified. Only He can refresh our spirit! Since that great day when I was baptized in the Holy Spirit I can say that God has a hold on me like never before. He has sealed me with his own Spirit and I know I am His forever. I am no longer afraid of God and the shame of my past is gone. I feel like such a different person, that at times I no longer recognize the previous me. Surely old things have passed away and the new has come. That deep depression has left never to return even in the midst of great loss. I have even tried to be depressed to see if it was really gone but I just can't. I guess when you are full of God's Spirit there isn't room for any of the things Satan has to offer. I am still learning more about God everyday. I know I still have a lot to learn but I thank God for the progress I have made. I believe the depression and struggles I have experienced were Satan's third attempt to destroy me. But I thank God He has a good plan for my life. A plan with a future and a hope! I have learned through it all, that God's grace is sufficient for me and that he will never leave me nor forsake me. Satan has no power over me and I look forward to the good things God has in store for His church"

Suzanne speaks of God having a good plan for her life, a plan that includes a future and a hope. God has a plan for us, that includes a hope that does not disappoint, a hope that does not fade away, like so many other things that we may go after, a hope that is not seen in material things, but brings blessing to our lives in ways that nothing else on earth can. Will we seek after that hope? Will we long for that hope? Are we willing to let go of our daily, grinding agenda, in order to spend time, seeking the hope of God. Let's take a look at the following verses in Romans, chapter 8:

Romans 8:18

> 18 For I consider that the sufferings of this present time are not worthy *to be compared* with the glory which shall be revealed in us.

There are times that I have greatly desired relief from the sufferings of this present time. I desired relief so much, that, at times, I have looked for ways of relief. Whether it was excessive television watching, over eating, or a host of other things, what I have discovered, is that, there just isn't anything that compares to the glory of God within a person. The "glory that is to be revealed in us" is the very presence of Jesus. We cannot fully comprehend how much He not only loves us, but also how much He desires to bless us, in this life and in the life to come. Things just go much better for us, in every regard, when we spend time seeking after Him. I'm not speaking of asking God for things, but rather, asking God for a revelation of Himself to us. Take a look:

From the Message Bible: Rom 8:19 The created world itself can hardly wait for what's coming next.

20 Everything in creation is being more or less held back. God reins it in.

21 until both creation and all the creatures are ready and can be released at the same moment into the glorious times ahead. Meanwhile, the joyful anticipation deepens.

22 All around us we observe a pregnant creation. The difficult times of pain throughout the world are simply birth pangs. But it's not only around us; it's within us. The Spirit of God is arousing us within. We're also feeling the birth pangs.

23 These sterile and barren bodies of ours are yearning for full deliverance.

24 That is why waiting does not diminish us, any more than waiting diminishes a pregnant

mother. We are enlarged in the waiting. We, of course, don't see what is enlarging us.

25 But the longer we wait, the larger we become, and the more joyful our expectancy.

26 Meanwhile, the moment we get tired in the waiting, God's Spirit is right alongside helping us along. If we don't know how or what to pray, it doesn't matter. He does our praying in and for us, making prayer out of our wordless sighs, our aching groans.

27 He knows us far better than we know ourselves, knows our pregnant condition, and keeps us present before God.

28 That's why we can be so sure that every detail in our lives of love for God is worked into something good.

There is a place in God that we can abide in, that is completely unrelated to our physical and emotional surroundings. Whatever is happening in your life at this very moment let me ask you, what is dominating your emotions? Are your feelings, and emotions, (your soulish realm), dominated by the circumstances of your physical, material life, and by the things that have happened, or that are happening to you? If so, it's time to change your focus. God is a Spirit, and we must worship Him in spirit and in truth. Our spirit needs to be continually making connection with God's Spirit. In that arena there is healing, blessing, love, freedom, victory, and sustenance.

Birth Pangs:

As I write today, it is the day after the disaster of hurricane Katrina hitting New Orleans, Biloxi MS, and Mobile Al as well as many other surrounding areas. The devastation is so horrendous that, even watching the news has been too much for me to stay with for very long. There seems to be increasing signs in the earth that all the things we see and know, are passing away. Several hurricanes hit Florida last year, then the Tsunami hit in the Indian Ocean, and now Katrina:

1 Thessalonians 5:2-6 (New Living Translation)

2 For you know quite well that the day of the Lord's return will come unexpectedly, like a thief in the night.

3 When people are saying, "Everything is peaceful and secure," then disaster will fall on them as suddenly as a pregnant woman's labor pains begin. And there will be no escape.

4 But you aren't in the dark about these things, dear brothers and sisters, and you won't be surprised when the day of the Lord comes like a thief.

5 For you are all children of the light and of the day; we don't belong to darkness and night.

6 So be on your guard, not asleep like the others. Stay alert and be clearheaded.

At this point, New Orleans is essentially no more. There is no commerce there. No electric, no water, no shipping, no banking, no buying, no selling, and almost no people. Martial law has been declared. The city has been evacuated. Several looters, and gangsters have been shot and killed. While the city most likely will open again in the near future, this event will never be forgotten by any of us. Many who had their hope in this life, are living today at the Astrodome, in Houston, or some other camp ground or facility in various parts of the U.S. I believe that the earth is in labor. I also believe that these labor pains will increase in frequency, and intensity, as they are even now. Jesus is coming again, and He is preparing for Himself a bride. A pure and holy bride will be focused, full of anticipation, and purpose. She will not be distracted with all the details of married life. She will be love struck. She will be shutting out all the distractions of mundane, and every day things, as she anticipates the coming of her beloved.

As hurricane Katrina accomplished its devastation, and as I have been watching the news day after day for the past week or so, with all of the gloominess, confusion, frustration, sadness, and loss, I began to feel, at first, depressed. I felt depressed to the point of not having any desire to read or hear the news any longer. There seems to be nothing else in the news, but this devastating event. At some point over the past week or so, I have begun to sense an anticipation, rather than feelings of depression. Why should my soul be downcast? Why should I be depressed? My joy is not dependent upon the price of gasoline, or upon the amount of any earthly possession that I am able to obtain, or hold on to. Everything in this life can, and will pass away. May it be now or at a future time, but now we can see and hear the pains of birth upon a pregnant earth. The earth itself, I believe, is in anticipation of the Second Coming of Christ Jesus.

Revelation 21 (New Living Translation)

1 Then I saw a new heaven and a new earth, for the old heaven and the old earth had disappeared. And the sea was also gone.

2 And I saw the holy city, the new Jerusalem, coming down from God out of heaven like a bride beautifully dressed for her husband.

3 I heard a loud shout from the throne, saying, "Look, God's home is now among his people! He will live with them, and they will be his people. God himself will be with them.

4 He will wipe every tear from their eyes, and there will be no more death or sorrow or crying or pain. All these things are gone forever."

5 And the one sitting on the throne said, "Look, I am making everything new!" And then he said to me, "Write this down, for what I tell you is trustworthy and true."

6 And he also said, "It is finished! I am the Alpha and the Omega—the Beginning and the End. To all who are thirsty I will give freely from the springs of the water of life." Also he said, "Write this down, for these words are trustworthy and true."

A holy bride is longing for intimacy with the bridegroom. She is thirsting for His attention, and affection. Jesus once said to His disciples, that He no longer called them servants, but friends. As children of God, and as the spiritual bride of Christ, we are called the friend of God. We must understand that God favors us! He longs for us, even as we long for Him. As you read these words, I want to take a moment to speak blessings over you. Right now, I declare that you are favored of God! I declare that you are not only favored, but also highly favored! As a person of faith, you are chosen. You are called out. You are in this world, but not of it. I pray that the Lord will, even at this very moment, lavish His love on you! I speak to your future days to be full of the purpose of God. Full of the destiny that Jesus has for you. I declare that every purpose of the enemy of your soul is defeated. No more of the past. No more of that which is done away with. I speak peace over your mind, your heart, and your soul. I declare anxiety and fear to be far removed from you. May the blessing of God overtake you. May your heart and mind be established in saturated desire for God. May hunger and thirst for God be your portion every day, from this day forward!

As children of God, we are recipients of His grace, and His gifts. Too much of the time, the church has thought of itself only as vessels to be used of God. That's good, but we cannot be fully used of God in displaying His great love, unless we are absolutely saturated *in* His great love. Jesus comes to Peter, to wash his feet, and Peter says No way! I won't let you do it. Jesus' reply is simple, but so powerful, "If I do not wash you, then you have no part with me." Peter immediately responded, "not only my feet then, but my hands, and my head as well."

A person can abuse their body in service for Jesus, and lose out on the most important thing of all... knowing Jesus. Paul said, "that I might know Him, and the power of His resurrection." Mary and Martha, two sisters who loved Jesus deeply, had two different views. Martha emphasized getting things done, but Mary, according to Jesus had "chosen the good part," as she sat at Jesus' feet and soaked in every word that He spoke. Let me ask you this, do you desire to work for God? There is coming a judgment day, when Christ will say to some, "Depart from me, I never knew you." On that day, He will not be saying, "Depart from me, you didn't do enough good deeds." Please don't misunderstand. We are created in Christ Jesus for good works, but the point of the whole matter, is that we be (reside) in Christ Jesus, and that He be in us, and that He knows us. The word "knows" in scripture, many times, implies intimacy. Jesus says to the Laodocian church, in Revelation chapter 2, "Behold, I stand at the door and knock. If anyone will open the door, I will come in to him, and sup with him, and he with me." So, the question is, do we impress God with our many faceted works? While we may impress men, we will not impress God. In fact, I do not believe that God is impressed with any thing that we do that is not connected to relationship with Him. Not anything at all! Visions and revelation came to Peter about what God would have him to do, not while he was out working for God, but while he was on a roof top seeking the face and heart of God. You will hear from God, and have clear direction for your life as you abide in a place of intimacy with Him.

Ps. 1, vs. 1-2 says, "Blessed is the man who walks not in the counsel of the ungodly, nor stands in the path of sinners, nor sits in the seat of the scornful; but his delight is in the law of the Lord. And in His law he meditates day and night." It goes on to say in verse 3 that this person who delights himself in the Lord, and meditates upon Him, is one who will bring forth fruit, and prosper in everything he does, just like a tree planted by the rivers of water. Flowing water, in scripture represents the moving of the Holy Spirit in our lives.

Ps. 23, vs. 1-3 says, "The Lord is my shepherd, He makes me to lie down in green pastures; He leads me beside the still waters. He restores my soul."

If you and I walk and live in this life, with a soul that is in constant desperate need of restoration because of the continual bombardment of the circumstances of life, then we will have very little to offer to others who are hurting and in need of Christ. That being said, we must walk in a position of being continually refreshed and restored in the presence of God. I encourage you to spend time in the secret place of the most high God. Spend time there alone. Spend time there with other people of like precious faith. Do not allow your soul to be full of despair, but rather allow the Holy Spirit to wash over you continually. You can do this by worshipping God, and by thanking Him daily for what He is doing, and is about to do in your life. When you talk with God, it should be a two-way conversation. He longs to sup with you, not just to instruct you or to reprimand you. In other words, He desires to tell you, by His Spirit, how much He loves you. In a marriage relationship, a couple is not successful by instructing each other every day, and pointing out faults. A bride is blessed with strength, as her husband speaks loving words over her continually. "You are so beautiful." "I love you so much." "I can't wait to see you." Saying things like this from the heart will not only bless a spouse, but will bless the marriage, and strengthen it. Many times, when temptation enters a marriage, it is because the couple has forsaken the intimate discussions of love that once brought them together, and the relationship has been reduced to becoming instructors and inspectors of one another. Then, Satan looking for an opportunity will provide some lonely, longing soul to bring words of love and sweetness. It is the same with our relationship with Father God. He is our Father. We are called His children. We are also called His bride. These are terms of intimacy. If you receive Christ, while sensing His love and desire for you, and then reduce that love to requirements and religious rules, then you have missed the mark. Jesus did what He did for us, because of love for us. He did it because He longs to be intimate with us. Ability to obey Him comes from His heart. It comes from His love. "God demonstrated His love for us, in that, while we were yet sinners, Christ died for us." There is nothing that He is waiting for you to do in order to draw close to you, except for you to desire Him. "Draw near to God, and He will draw near to you." "Behold I stand at the door and knock, if anyone opens the door, I will come in and sup with Him, and he with me."

Jesus said that the Kingdom of God does not come with observation. In other words, it is not an earthly kingdom. It is heavenly, and supernatural. He further said that His kingdom was within us who are believers. The Kingdom of God, which is within every believer, is far more powerful than any earthly kingdom. By the power of God's kingdom on earth, Jesus cast out demons, healed the sick, and raised the dead, demonstrating that His kingdom greatly outweighs Satan's kingdom on this earth. What we must do is to become much more aware of God's kingdom within us, by seeking His kingdom first, and putting His kingdom before all things.

The enemy of your soul will do anything and everything within his power to distract you from God's kingdom. Why? Because God's kingdom that is alive within you, will tear down the strongholds of Satan in you as well as those around you. I've heard it said that Satan has the "weapons of mass distraction." He would rather you do anything, stay as busy as you can possibly imagine, or as distracted as you can get, as long as you and I are not seeking first the kingdom of God. You and I are no threat to the strongholds that hold our friends, associates, and loved ones captive, unless we are firmly aware of, and saturated with the kingdom of God within us. A kingdom must have a king. The word kingdom means "the king's domain." If we are seeking first the kingdom of God, then we are seeking the king of that kingdom. There is nothing you could do that will please God more than seeking Him, His will, and His kingdom. "Thy kingdom come, thy will be done ON EARTH as it is in heaven." Scripture also says in the same portion, "Give us THIS DAY, our daily bread." There is really nothing for us to be distracted with, when our eyes are fixed on Jesus. When our trust and hope are fully in God, we have no need of worrying about tomorrow's troubles, because we are seeking God daily for that day's bread. Jesus gives seed to the sower. He is our daily bread.

Merkel was a place of learning, and growing in the knowledge and understanding of spiritual warfare. I'll never forget asking the Lord one night to expose every hidden and secret thing in the church. After that night, it seemed that the bowels and depths of demonically inspired things in people began to erupt in the forms of false accusations, rebellion in leaders, and so forth. During our 11 years at Merkel, we had just about every type of rebellion in leadership that you can imagine.

I do not believe that God will speak to His children to disrespect and disobey a direct request from their Pastor regarding spiritual and church ministry issues. Pride is the root of many of these areas of our lives that are kept from God. Pride will continually keep a person clinging to things that please the flesh, things that attract attention to ourselves, instead of to Christ, and keep us from God's best for us. I believe that God greatly longs to reveal Himself to us. I believe that He greatly longs to speak to us by His Spirit. When He does, we will inevitably say, as John did, "I must decrease, He must increase."

Pastoring people, we were finding out, was no easy task. I began to feel, at times, as though I could not give a word of instruction to anyone other than from the pulpit, and then I must be very careful to keep things extremely general, so as not to hint of referring to any particular situation in the church. A study of the Apostle Paul's writings demonstrates that this is not biblical, and that at times, serious issues had to be dealt with, individually, and sometimes publicly. One thing about rebellion and disunity being exposed is that it will drive a Pastor to a desperate place, and he may either cry out to God for revival, or else give up. Many things that God desires to deal with in our hearts may never be dealt with, if those things remain hidden. God desires to deal with our heart issues, because He desires us, and not our outward appearance of righteousness. The Pastor is in need of God's grace and daily presence no less than any other person. Being a Pastor is only a position in the church that is appointed and anointed by God. It is not a position of greater freedom from flesh and struggle than others. I believe this is where Pastors blow it at times, in public speaking. Why should I not recognize before the congregation that I have the exact same desperate need of the overcoming power of the Spirit as anyone listening to me? I am not able to help people from the pulpit by showing off my "righteous goodness. We are all flesh and blood until we get to heaven. If we portray anything otherwise, (in any position of ministry), then we are failing miserably. During our 11 years of pastoring and living at Merkel Texas, Rebekah and I faced some of the most trying times in our marriage, and in our family and lives that we have ever faced. My goal in writing here is not in sharing every detail of those struggles, but rather in demonstrating the grace, love, and absolute ability of God to bring us through any of life's circumstances. Satan attacked our marriage and our relationship began to suffer. I can tell you that today our marriage relationship is stronger than ever. I will say, as Paul said, "I do not set aside the grace of God." If my right standing with God or with my wife for that matter came by works, then Christ died in vain. Jesus makes my love for my wife greater than I alone could ever make it. It is the flesh, the soulish realm of man that creates so much havoc and disaster. We are in the world, but not of the world, scripture declares. We will always have flesh until we get to heaven, but at the same time we have a heavenly kingdom that has invaded earth. We have access to that kingdom. We must stay in tune with God's kingdom. There is no way to remain in tune with His kingdom without seeking the king of that kingdom.

When God sends revival to a church, it is not because the Pastor, or a particular intercessor is more spiritual than others, but rather God sees desire, longing, and hears the heart cry from the pulpit to the pew of people who desire liberty, freedom, and His ability helping us. He sends revival because people long for Him, desire Him, and come after Him. Some are intercessors; some are grounds keepers by gifting and calling. All of us must be seekers of God, and do that with a humble heart. With a heart that understands that we are unwise to compare ourselves by ourselves. All of us have different gifts and talents. One writes songs, another constructs buildings, another is gifted in organization, etc. One key factor I believe, in God sending revival, is that people support the vision of their Pastor and church, rather than looking for the church to support their vision. God will always make room for every person's gift and talent, as they submit to the local church vision and mission. At Merkel I began crying out to God for revival, not because I was spiritual, but rather because I was hurting and realized that I could do nothing without Him. People were not going to follow my leadership because I had the title of Pastor. I needed more of God's grace and anointing. People needed healing, they needed God's love; they needed real messages of hope. This type of blessing from God would not come by "revival meetings" but by a visitation from heaven.

Chapter 8

WHEN THE HOLY SPIRIT VISITS YOU

During our 11 years at Merkel, we witnessed several very powerful times of God's visitation. One lasted 9 weeks, and another 11 weeks. I'll never forget when a good friend of mine, Pastor Paul Vincent, came in to preach on a Sunday for us. There was an unusual sense of the presence of God that day, and after the evening service, during the altar call time, I whispered to him, "Would you be able to stay for Monday night?" He immediately said yes, and so it began. On Monday night, the Holy Spirit filled us, and I asked "Can you stay for Tuesday night?" "Yes" was his reply, and that turned into Wednesday night, and continued for the next 11 weeks. During that time, there was a woman coming each night, whose husband, Frank, thought that his wife was seeing another man. "Nobody attends church every night of the week." he thought. One night he came intending to spy on his wife, and sit in the back. When he arrived, he noticed his wife sitting alone, and went and sat next to her. That night, during the altar call for salvation, Frank was the first to step forward, and ask Jesus into his life, to be his Savior. Frank, at the time, had long hair, and a countenance that was unmistakably sad. The next night, Frank was there again, except this time, he was literally unrecognizable as the same person. He had been so gloriously changed, as he had allowed the Holy Spirit to look deep inside of him, that his face literally looked like a completely different person. Frank, who could not understand why his wife would be at church every night, suddenly, after having an awesome encounter with the Holy Spirit, was now someone that you couldn't keep away from the church. He began volunteering to help in any and every capacity. Frank ultimately became our church maintenance and grounds keeper, and could be found at the church on just about any day of the week (I miss you Frank).

When God looks inside of us, He not only sees what's wrong, but as we open the door to Him, He heals what's wrong, and many times He does this work very quickly. I've heard it said, that when someone is on the church carpet, shaking, or displaying some sort of manifestation in the Holy Spirit, that there should be a "red light flashing, and a sign that says, God at work." The outward manifestation, that so many people seem to shy away from, or be afraid of, is simply a sign of an inward work of the Holy Spirit of God.

The outward manifestation is not something to put confidence in, anymore than having confidence in a surgeon's knife. While the knife may reveal a manifestation in the body, the surgeon is doing the work to bring about a healing process. So many today are carrying hurts, unforgiveness, resentment, hatred, bitterness, envy, etc. towards other people. And although it may be justified in a person's mind, these attributes will only devastate and destroy the ones who carry them. When God moves in an individual, He fills them with love. He forgives their sins, and washes away iniquity. At the same time, in order for complete healing, He requires that we forgive those who've sinned against us. We must even, and perhaps especially, forgive ourselves. No one knows our sins and weaknesses more than we know them ourselves. If we do not forgive, God says that we will not be forgiven. Forgiveness on our part must not require that the one who offended us ask forgiveness. In fact, our forgiving others must not require anything of them, just as Christ taking our sin on the cross had no requirement of us. Although you may not deserve what others have done to you, in hurting you, we must realize that we live in a fallen state of being, and everyone in this state is in need of grace and mercy. If you feel that someone owes you an apology, then you are not walking in forgiveness toward that person. In other words, there must not be any requirement on our part, in order for us to forgive another. If they do apologize, then they receive something of benefit for themselves, but their apology does not offer you the right to forgive. It is vitally important that we cast down our judgments of others, and walk in love as believers. There is nothing biblically accurate, or spiritually accurate, that says that someone owes us something before we can forgive them. If we do not forgive, then we will not be forgiven by God. This plan of God is for our blessing, and I believe that something we must realize as believers and know is that God does all things for our benefit. When we love, and forgive unconditionally, then we receive an abundance of forgiveness and blessing from God.

During our 9 week revival with Jim and Anita Maxell, we had some incredible visitations from the Holy Spirit. On one of those revival nights, I'll never forget that as I was leading worship and sensing the awesome presence of the Holy Spirit, I didn't feel that I could stand any longer. There was no one standing behind me to catch me, as I felt I was about to fall backwards, so I grabbed the pulpit, which offered almost nothing in the way of holding me up, so I let go, turned, and fell on my face on the platform. When this happened, there was an extreme quiet that came over the congregation. I lay motionless, pretty much unable to move or even open my eyes for about 40 minutes. During this time I heard nothing. Not a child talking, not a person coughing... nothing! After a while I wanted to look around and see what was going on, and as I slowly lifted my head and turned to the piano, I saw Rebekah lying under it. I looked back at our drummer, Dave, and he was on the floor next to the drums. I then looked out toward the congregation, and people were laid out everywhere. Some were draped over pews; others were under pews, or on the floor next to them. No one was groaning, moaning, shaking, or anything like that. Everyone was just peaceful and quiet. I then turned my attention to our evangelist, and he was still sitting on the pew on the platform. As I looked to him, I was beginning to become a little worried about such a long time of quiet, and nothing happening, and thought that I better have him go ahead and preach. As I motioned to Jim to come to the pulpit, he thought that I was motioning for him to come and pick me up. As he attempted to do so, he fell off the pew and onto the floor on his face. For the next 2 hours he lay there, and when the service "ended" we picked him up, and helped him to his travel trailer. He did not speak to us, nor was he apparently able to until the next day. So, although this all sounds surreal, and very odd, there is a purpose for this. And that purpose, regardless of the manifestation at the time, is that God loves people, and desires to set them free from anxiety, fear, depression, ungodliness, mental battles, etc., etc. And when His Spirit invades a church service in this fashion, God is saying, in essence, "I'm here, and I long to have true intimacy with you, and not just another ritualistic meeting." He's saying "I love my people, and will comfort, strengthen, and establish you." I have experienced similar manifestations before this, especially during my late teen years after I had sensed the call to preach, but never with so many people all at the same time. I love the way God loves us and will surprise us with joy, hope, love, and healing when we may be expecting something ordinary.

Chapter 9

BECOMING RECHARGED AND RENEWED

During our last year at Merkel, I began to know deep down, that God had released me from pastoring there, and that it was time to move on. "To everything there is a season…" I really had no desire to pastor a different church, and many times, said to Rebekah, "If I'm going to be a Pastor somewhere else, then I will just stay here." She would agree, and we'd cast the thought aside for while. The trouble was that God was beginning to compel me to move on. When we allow the Holy Spirit to look inside of us, it must be continuing and ongoing. It is something that we grow deeper in, as time goes by. Following the Holy Spirit's lead is a life long commitment. At any rate, when I would be locking up the church after services, I would think "I'm out of here." The Spirit of God, I realize now, was compelling these thoughts. He was making me uncomfortable in my longstanding comfortable position. Our children had had their entire schooling in the Merkel ISD. We had enjoyed years of sports and other community activities with our children, and it was simply a comfortable place to continue in, except for the prompting and agitation of the Spirit of God. I had stated a number of times, that if I were to leave Merkel I would never again be involved in a church building program, and that I would never be a senior Pastor again. I knew that I could not leave the ministry, but also knew that I could serve as Evangelist, or as an Assistant Pastor in a larger church. Many times, however, my thoughts were full of complaints and greatly lacking in faith.

Something that is very important for us to understand is that we do not get anything from God by manipulation. We get nothing from God by how hurt we are, or by how confused we are, or by how disappointed we are in others. We get nothing from God by complaining, but only by faith and thankfulness. Our peace from God is not dependent upon how others have failed us, or how they have treated us. It has nothing to do with our circumstances. God is always the same. He's always ready to give us joy, and peace, and is full of tenderheartedness towards us. He does not demonstrate His love toward us, and manifest His presence in us because we "can't take it anymore." He never responds favorably to complaints or fear, or anxiety. He only responds favorably to faith. "Without faith it is impossible to please God." Although He may keep us from drowning when we cry out to Him in fear, His peace and joy will only infuse our lives as a result of our faith and trust in Him.

Faith has nothing to do with what we think about others, or how we think they should act, or what we feel others should be doing. Faith trusts and submits to what God is doing, and what He is yet to do. People quit and give up many times, not because of what or who God is, or what they see Him doing, but because of how they perceive that others have failed them, or their perception of how God has let them down. If God tells you to build a boat, and no one helps except your wife and kids, you build the boat rejoicing all the while. You and God are a majority. If God tells you to free 6 million people from the hand of Pharaoh, you go, regardless of how unkindly you may be received. That's genuine faith and trust in God, and His ability within us. That same faith keeps you steadfast in the desert when there is no water and no bread. Faith doesn't focus on the how, but on complete trust in God.

There is such peace, such joy, and such over-whelming grace in the midst of God's presence in you. He always hears and answers your cry when you believe in Him. If you have failed God, and grieved His Holy Spirit, know that there is nothing you can physically do to make it up to Him. He loves you, and renews your mind because you trust in His Word. We seem to try so hard to please God with our efforts, and yet God has already told us, "Without faith, it is impossible to please Him…" Scripture says that He died for us, "while we were yet sinners." While grace is no license for sin, at the same time we must understand that as long as we are in this body we are subject to shortcomings. God sees no sin in you because, by your faith, Jesus is in you. Whenever we base our walk with God on our performance, we will only become discouraged, and feel the condemnation of the enemy of our souls. Satan is the accuser of the brethren and he will find plenty of areas to accuse you. So our hope is always in the covenant of our Saviors blood. Hebrews 10:10 tells us that we are sanctified through the body of Jesus once and for all time. I'm not suggesting that it is impossible for a saved person to lose his/her salvation, but what I am saying is that our salvation is always faith based, and never works based. Scripture says that "Godly sorrow…leaves no regret." When we sorrow over something we may have done that we know is not pleasing to God, and if that sorrow is brought on by the Spirit of God that is working within us, then we will not ever give up but rather submit ourselves to the only answer that really works, and that is the same grace that saved us to begin with. Grace is God's ability in me. While grace is not a license to sin, it is also not a one time gift for the day of your salvation. Grace is an ongoing process that continues working in us throughout our lifetime.

Everything we do is all about Him, and not about us, not about how we feel or how others respond to us. I've never seen someone quit a church or a ministry because of what God was doing. Whatever I face, whoever agrees or disagrees, even when it seems my ministry is nowhere close to meeting my expectations and hopes, I can still find absolute joy in Him. Nothing else matters without His presence, His peace, and His joy abiding within us. "Unless the Lord builds the house, they labor in vain who build it." It's not about getting our will, but rather about fulfilling His will, and His will cannot be accomplished in us without faith. Faith brings us into the realm of seeking God diligently, and diligently seeking God brings about rewards. "He is a rewarder of those who diligently seek Him." Scripture does not tell us that He is a rewarder of those who can compare themselves in a better light than others.

Chapter 10

HEARING AND KNOWING GOD'S DIRECTION

About a year before I left Merkel, I took a few church leaders and attended a ministry conference in Oklahoma. Pastor Steve Gray (World Revival Church) (Formerly, or also known as the Smithton Outpouring), was one of the speakers. After he spoke, I felt compelled to share with him my agony, thoughts of despair, and feelings of being at the end of my time at Merkel. I told him that I didn't know what to do, or where to go. After I shared this with him I said, "I don't know why I'm sharing this with you." and he replied, "I do. I would like for you to consider becoming a staff member, as an associate Pastor at our church." I was overjoyed to hear this. I had expected a word of encouragement, and possibly a prayer for clear direction, but this, this was more than I could have dreamed of hearing him say. This was my chance to be free. Free from bearing the heavy load of being the Senior Pastor in a small church. This was, in my mind, a chance to see my ministry, and my calling grow, a chance to observe from the inside, how a large successful ministry operated, without having to organize it myself. My ministry, to this point, seemed to contain my God-given vision of preaching the Word, but was without my expected and sought after results of developing into a "big church ministry." I was very willing to be faithful in my calling regardless of the "results," but at the same time, I was somewhat disillusioned by the results, or what I considered to be the lack of results. Based my past experience of accomplished ministries in the churches I had grown up in, success was measured in numbers, the bigger the numbers the greater the success. I have since come to understand that it is not the size or amount of ministry that is important to God, but simply a willing and obedient heart.

An obedient heart will always attract the favor and blessing of God. To fear the Lord, simply put, is to obey Him. When we walk as obedient children, we need not concern ourselves with so called results, but rather trust the "Lord of the Harvest." We are used of God in the harvest field, but He is the Lord of this harvest. He places each of us in the body according to His will and purpose. The amount of "results" that we personally witness is not for us to question or to concern ourselves with when we walk in surrender to the will of God, and obedience to that will. I had been willing to obey the Lord since he set me on fire as a teen. But when I was a teen, I was set on fire in an atmosphere of BIG church mentality. I knew nothing else in my past experience to relate or measure "success," hence it was extremely difficult, if not impossible, for me to feel a sense of contentedness without seeing an explosion of growth taking place. In reality, we actually had wonderful success, and many blessed and productive programs, considering the small town we were in. In a town of 2,400 people, with a predominant population of Baptists, Methodists, and Church of Christ raised people, we had seen our congregation grow from 15 to 120 people. We had established an outreach center in the heart of downtown Merkel, feeding and clothing people. We had knocked on every door in Merkel, praying with hundreds of people over the years. We had seen miraculous healings, salvations, and discipleship take place, and still I was not content with the results. From the time the Lord called me into ministry, I envisioned thousands coming to Christ. I envisioned a much bigger ministry than what I had so far experienced. Now, there I was, standing before Pastor Steve Gray, and he was directing me to his son-in-law in order to begin a process of interview, and resume examination.

Although I was excited, Rebekah was not nearly as comforted by the idea of moving to Kansas City as I was. She had always followed me wherever I felt led to go, and I knew that this would be no different. This excitement I was sensing, however, was in my flesh, and not in my spirit. This was not something that I had spent time praying and seeking the Lord's will about, but I didn't care. I simply believed that this opportunity was an answer to all the prayers and cries of the past few months. When we returned home, I immediately sent my resume, and began interviewing over the phone with Pastor Grays son-in-law. Everything looked like a go. Pastor Gray and I were now e-mailing back and forth, and the only possible hindrance was a man that had been interviewed for the position before me. I had been told that he was not going to be able to make the move, or something along those lines, so I wasn't worried about it. I felt that I had the job. During this process, a dear friend of mine, Pastor Paul Vincent, had resigned his position at Harvest Assembly of God, in Georgetown, Texas, and had taken a Pastorate at another church in South Texas. I had preached revival meetings at the Georgetown church, and was familiar with the people. I knew that the people there were wonderful, and had been under great leadership for the past 10 years. At the same time, I had no interest in applying for the position as Pastor at Georgetown for a number of reasons. First of all, they had purchased land, and were in great need of a new building. Secondly, the building they were in needed to be sold, and the prospects of selling it didn't seem very likely to me. In addition to these things, I had no desire to be involved in another building project, nor did I desire to live in Georgetown. Funny, funny, the Lord has a sense of humor, and definitely works in mysterious ways. As I type these words, I am the Pastor of Harvest A/G, Georgetown, TX, and I'm living in a parsonage on the 12 acres where the new church is now being constructed. Okay, I'm getting ahead of myself. There I was, waiting to hear that I had been hired at WRC in Kansas City, when I found myself on the phone with one of the board members, Glen Hawks, from Georgetown. I knew this man to be a man of God, a man who was sensitive to the Spirit of God, and a man who heard from God regularly. I had great respect for this man. On the phone we were discussing the potential of me coming to Pastor the church at Georgetown, and I'm telling Glenn that I believe I will be moving to Kansas City. Then I hear these words over the phone from Glenn, "You're not going to Kansas City." WHAT!? I thought, why would he say something like this to me? I've been praying, begging, interceding for my future, and the future of my wife and kids. I have no intention of being in an old building, when I have a very nice building and congregation right where I am. The whole purpose in leaving Merkel was to no longer be a senior Pastor. My thoughts were racing, but I knew that Glenn was a man of God. The next morning, as I opened my e-mail, there it was, an e-mail from Pastor Steve Gray, saying that the first man they had interviewed had decided to take the position, and that he was sorry for any inconvenience that he have caused me. The Lord was again directing our steps, Glenn had heard from God, and I was to be the next Pastor of the small congregation in Georgetown, Texas.

Following the leading and guiding of the Holy Spirit requires faith. My circumstances told me that I was finished as a Senior Pastor. God said no. The Lord directing my steps to Georgetown, and me continuing to Pastor did not mean that I was free from baggage, from hurt and confusing thoughts. There were battles that Rebekah and I had gone through at Merkel that I have not mentioned in this book. The relevance in relating some of those struggles is found in the fact that our marriage is stronger than ever, and that we have been and are still being sustained by the grace and love of God. A Pastor, just as any other member of the body of Christ, must not live to please people and to fulfill their expectations, but to please God, and knowing that His yoke is easy. This was one of the battles that I greatly struggled with. Perhaps because I had faced what I perceived to be a great deal of rejection growing up, I had a fear of letting people down. I wanted people to believe in me. I had feelings of insecurity. Many times, after preaching, I would lay in bed at night thinking, "I blew it. Why did I say this, or that." "Why wasn't Joe at church, or Mary?" "What have I done to offend them?" I would beat myself up over unrealistic expectations of myself, or by what I perceived others expected of me. In the pulpit I was bold. I had no problem delivering the Word of God without watering it down, and had no fear of what people might like or dislike when it came to my preaching ministry, but for whatever reason, this boldness didn't always translate clearly into my ministry and life outside the pulpit. People, who would get to know me in advance of hearing me preach, would inevitably say after hearing me preach things like, "I couldn't believe that was the same person." or "Wow, what a difference." The positive side of this was that I was not an offensive person in public, however the negative was that it was extremely difficult and uncomfortable for me to confront negative situations outside of the pulpit. Many, many times, I would hold things inside that needed to be confronted, hoping and praying and believing that God was going to work it out. At times things would work themselves out, but for the times that confrontation was necessary, it was not only difficult for me, but I began to have panic attacks over the situations.

During one such attack, during a service at Merkel, I simple got up while a guest speaker was preaching and left the building. I went home and paced the floor, unable to even sit down. Rebekah came home asking "Are you okay?" I wasn't. Things escalated and I would refuse to answer the phone, or the door. I felt that I could not meet the expectations of others, and that feeling was too much for me to handle because of the fear of rejection. Fear of rejection and fear of man is a terrible thing that can bind a person, and prevent him/her from developing their potential in life. Something else that the Lord would teach me over time was that my calling was to minister to people, and not to "fix" them. A friend of mine, Jim Maxwell, shared with me of how, as a Pastor the Holy Spirit spoke to his heart... "What are you doing." He replied, "I'm trying to fix your people." The Lords response to Jim was along these lines... "I've called you to minister to my people, not to fix them." Only God, who created us can fix us.

What we must know and understand first is that God accepts us truly, just as we are. Just as we are on the day when we accepted him as Lord of our life, and just as we are the day after that, and just as we are 10 years later, and just as we are for the rest of our lives. This is a walk of faith and trust in God. It is not a walk of faith and trust in man. People let us down, and what too often happens is that we begin to see God through the eyes of men, instead of seeing men through the eyes of God. God is not a man. Man, although created in the image of God, is living in a fallen state. We truly must see people through the eyes of the Spirit of God. God is love. God is gentle. God is kind. God is forgiving, compassionate, and tender-hearted towards us. God is also not panicky. He is not afraid of man, and He is not afraid of the Devil. He is not afraid to confront, because He is completely secure in who He is. As we walk in faith and trust in God, knowing that He is living within us, we become secure. We discover that we can be bold, strong, and without fear, simply because it is no longer we who live, but Christ who lives within us. Remember God is love, and His love is perfect. "Perfect love casts out fear."

Chapter 11

LOVE IS THE KEY

The more of God's love you and I can be filled with, the more secure we will become. Encouragement from others is good, but as believers in Christ, our affirmation of who we are must come from the presence of God within us. Scripture says, "As a man thinks in his heart, so is he." If your heart's thoughts are focused on Jesus, focused on His love and the good plan He has for you, then you will not fail to receive God's best for your life. Look at these verses:

Hebrews 12:2

> 2 looking unto Jesus, the author and finisher of our faith, who for the joy that was set before Him endured the cross…"

The joy set before Jesus when He endured the cross was you. It was relationship and intimacy with you and me. Look to Him who not only authored your faith, but is finishing the work. When you got saved, God wasn't finished with His work in you. The "just" do not simply get saved by faith, the just live by faith. "The Just shall live by faith." In other words, you can not be just if you do not live by faith. Faith is all about focus. Focus on Jesus; focus on the Word of God. Keeping our eyes fixed on Him.

Proverbs 3:5-6
>   5   Trust in the LORD with all your heart,
>   And lcan not on your own understanding;
>   6   In all your ways acknowledge Him,
>   And He shall direct your paths.

Stop leaning to what the world has taught you to believe about God, and begin to see Him inside of you. See Him living in you, and through you, rather than you trying to please Him with your own efforts. Religious activity does not attract the blessing and favor of God, but rather faith and trust in God does.

Hebrews 10:38-39
>   38   *"Now the just shall live by faith;*
>   *But if anyone draws back,*
>   *My soul has no pleasure in him."*
>   39   But we are not of those who draw back to perdition, but of those who believe to the saving of the soul.

Some will inevitably read these verses and think that God is not pleased with us because we are not behaving well enough, but this is not what God is saying to us. He is saying that He takes no pleasure in the one who draws back away from faith. Because Christ fulfilled the law of commandments for us, it is only Christ who can keep us in a state of freedom, and we cannot remain in Christ by trying harder. Our own understanding will lead us to trying harder to please God. The fact is, it is not trying that God is pleased with in us. It is Jesus that God is pleased with in us. You could not, and cannot ever pay any portion of the price for your salvation.

The children of Israel who did not make it into the Promised Land, did not enter because of their unbelief, according to Hebrews 3:19.

In verse 18 scripture says "to whom did He swear that they would not enter His rest, but to those who did not obey?"

It was unbelief that caused them to disobey God. Obedience to God is non-existent without faith in God. Scripture says, "Faith without works is dead." The truth of this verse is that when you and I have faith and live by faith in God, we cannot continue in disobedience. "The just shall live by faith." I've had people say to me… "I've tried God. It just didn't work for me. I felt nothing, I didn't experience what others experienced." My response these days is this.. "Don't tell me you've tried God until after you're dead." Faith in God is not based solely on experience, but rather trust in God. Job, in the midst of tremendous personal tragedy, said in faith, "The Lord gives and the Lord takes away, blessed be the name of the Lord."

As I write today, I am in Nashville, Tennessee, where record heat has been affecting the area. Yesterday, as we drove past a local church, the sign outside read – "You think it's hot here!" The implication being that hell is waiting. While fear of hell may convince some to come to Christ for salvation, fear of hell will not keep people living for God. You see, people are going to follow the nature that has been given to them. We are born with a sin nature, and we will abide by that nature until we take on a different nature. God desires to give us His nature. The only way for that to happen is through relationship with Him that comes by faith in Him. We do not get His nature because we are afraid of Him. Fear of God is not the same as being afraid of God. True Godly fear is that which has us trusting God, trusting His presence, trusting His peace and trusting His joy. The children of Israel, while in the desert were afraid of God, but lost their faith in God. It was that loss of faith that kept them from the Promised Land.

Let's look at 2 Peter 1:3-4 (New Living Translation)

3 By his divine power, God has given us everything we need for living a godly life. *We have received all of this by coming to know him*, the one who called us to himself by means of his marvelous glory and excellence.

4 And because of his glory and excellence, he has given us great and precious promises. These are the promises that enable you to share his divine nature and escape the world's corruption caused by human desires

Remember that "faith comes by hearing, and hearing by the Word of God." I recently heard it said. "Faith does not come to us by having heard, but by hearing the Word." I've spoken with people who say – "I've heard the Word. I heard it every week, and memorized many verses, and it did nothing for me." Let's hear what God is saying to us in His Word. I'd like to suggest a few words to associate with "hearing the Word"—Words like receive – welcome – adhere – accept – apply – say – do – walk in. First of all, according to the verses above, everything we need for living a godly life is given to us by God's divine power. Secondly, we receive God's divine power (grace) by coming to know Him. Third, I notice that the One that we are coming to know is the One who called us to Himself by means of His glory and excellence, and not our own. And because of HIS excellence, he has provided promises for us that will enable us to share in His divine nature and escape the world's corruption.

The promises are found in His Word. When people say "I've heard the Word and it didn't work for me," they are either deceived, or they lack understanding. The Word of God cannot fail us, because it is God's Word to us, and He cannot fail to live up to His Word. If He says in His Word that He will give His Holy Spirit to those who ask, then that is exactly what He will do for everyone who asks. I have spoken with atheists, who said, "Okay, I'll ask right now…" and then go on in a mocking tone to ask God for the Holy Spirit. Their objective is in proving God a liar, and a false God. They will receive nothing, and can receive nothing good from God in that context because they do not ask in faith. Scripture says in James 4:3, "You ask and receive not, because you ask amiss that you may consume it upon your lusts."

The greatest command for us to follow, within the promises of God's Word, is that we love the Lord our God with all our heart, mind, soul and strength. Love fulfills all the law. The problem many Christians have is that they have long forgotten about the love, the intimacy, the fellowship of the Spirit, and the liberty that comes with that, and have begun walking in a more legalistic view of God. The problem the atheist has is that he/she doesn't believe God, and (the ones I've met) desire to make a point that He doesn't exist. When people tell me that they've tried God and it didn't work for them, my reply is this: "You didn't try God!" "Try God and let me know how it worked out after you're dead." Trying God is not like trying different churches and deciding which one suits you. Truly "trying" God would be along the lines of what His word says about trying Him, and not our feeble attempts at selfish gain.

Malachi 3:14-17 (NLT)

14 "You have said, 'What's the use of serving God? What have we gained by obeying his commands or by trying to show the LORD of Heaven's Armies that we are sorry for our sins?

15 From now on we will call the arrogant blessed. For those who do evil get rich, and those who dare God to punish them suffer no harm.'"

16 Then those who feared the LORD spoke with each other, and the LORD listened to what they said. In his presence, a scroll of remembrance was written to record the names of those who feared him and always thought about the honor of his name.

17 "They will be my people," says the LORD of Heaven's Armies. "On the day when I act in judgment, they will be my own special treasure. I will spare them as a father spares an obedient child. 18 Then you will again see the difference between the righteous and the wicked, between those who serve God and those who do not."

If you are reading this book and thinking "I've tried God. I gave my life to Him and nothing happened. I never felt His presence. I never had Him to direct my steps, and overwhelm me with His peace and blessing." I would suggest to you that, while you may believe you've given God a chance, it's not a chance that you must give Him. He's not really looking for you to try Him out like a puppy that you have control over, but to trust Him as Lord over your life. He will lead, guide and direct the steps, pathway, and life, of every single person who commits themselves to Him with reckless abandon. He will manifest himself to the person who says, "I'll never let go of you, and you will never let go of me." Someone who proclaims, "I am my beloveds, and He is mine, His banner over me is love." He promised that He would never leave you or forsake you. The question is, who/what do you believe? Do you believe the philosophy that you have learned from this world? Do you believe thoughts that say, "God has forsaken me, God doesn't care about speaking to me, God really isn't there at all." When a person comes to God in faith, believing Him and says "I love you God. I accept Jesus' sacrifice for me. I confess you as my Savior and the Lord of my life," that person is making a lifelong commitment to the One who will empower them to live a life of contentment, joy, peace, and fulfillment.

Chapter 12

FINDING THE SECRET PLACE WITH GOD

Anyone who says they are completely fulfilled without Christ is living a lie. God created us for fellowship with Him. He did not create us for judgment, but for intimacy. The lies that people learn from the philosophy of this world can be ripped apart by the love and the power of God that every one of us can attain, simply by calling on Him in faith, and declaring, "Nothing will ever change my mind, this world is temporary, and my life in God is eternal." In order to keep the presence of God directing us daily, we must keep the Word of God in our constant and continual hearing. Remember, "Faith comes by hearing, and hearing by the Word of God." That you read the Bible means nothing, unless you continue to hide His Word in your heart. "Thy Word have I hid in my heart, that I might not sin against thee." David said.

So we see that we need God's nature, and we have that. We need God's weapons (which are not earthly), and we have those weapons. There is no more argument left. So what do we do when tragedy comes? Blame God? No way! He is not to blame, and cannot be worthy of any blame of any kind. He is blameless. "Let God be true, and every man a liar." The question is, how do we relate to God? Will we trust Him with absolute reckless abandon? This world is not eternal, but our relationship with Jesus IS eternal. So, what do we do with all the arguments? Cast them down. We must lay hold of the power of God by faith, and when we do so, we will have His ability in us to demolish all the lies against God. If your argument states, "I've tried God, and it didn't work." then you go back to the Word and HEAR it. Remember, it's not what you've heard in the past, it's what you hear the Word saying right now. Never stop hearing and heeding the Word and you will never lose your walk with God.

In scripture Paul says:

2 Cor. 10:3-6 (Message)

3-6 The world is unprincipled. It's dog-eat-dog out there! The world doesn't fight fair. But we don't live or fight our battles that way—never have and never will. The tools of our trade aren't for marketing or manipulation, but they are for demolishing that entire massively corrupt culture. We use our powerful God-tools for smashing warped philosophies, tearing down barriers erected against the truth of God, fitting every loose thought and emotion and impulse into the structure of life shaped by Christ. Our tools are ready at hand for clearing the ground of every obstruction and building lives of obedience into maturity.

2 Cor. 10:3-5 (NLT)

3 We are human, but we don't wage war as humans do.

4 We use God's mighty weapons, not worldly weapons, to knock down the strongholds of human reasoning and to destroy false arguments.

5 We destroy every proud obstacle that keeps people from knowing God.

Whenever we lean to our own understanding of things, we negate the power of God to act on our behalf. As you walk in Christ, nothing really matters outside of knowing Him. In other words, your walk with God is not determined by how Christians behave toward you, how others have treated you, or by what tragedies have happened in your life. Nothing matters except that He loves you, and He will always love you. In the parable of the Prodigal Son, the son thought things would be better for him away from the Father. He had good times, but in the end he needed his Father, and he thought to himself, "It would be better for me to live with the

servants of my Father, than to live like I'm living."
He didn't know or comprehend that his Father would
not only welcome him home, but also would lavish
love and blessings on him. God isn't looking at this
moment to punish us. He is looking to fill us with
blessings unspeakable, and love that will rock your
world. Believing and trusting Him is the key. God is
not what we've imagined Him to be, and yet people
continue to avoid coming "home" to Him.

At this point, I am at a place where the things that
really count in my life are my relationship with my
family, my friends and church family, and with Jesus.
Without closeness to Jesus I would not be who I am.
I would not be able to walk in the joy that I currently
have with my wife and family.

Our church in Georgetown, TX is currently in a
construction project for a new building. This project
is implementing volunteers for much of the work.
There have been ups and downs, disagreements, and
differences in opinion about styles of ministry, differences of opinion about the building itself, and financial struggles during this period. We had our church
services in a tent on the property for over a year, with
extreme heat, and extreme cold. Some told me "People
won't stay. You won't make it." but not only did we
make it, the church has continued to grow under the
tent. Our building is still, at this point unfinished,
although we are now meeting in the partially finished
fellowship hall. In all the struggle of Pastoring people,
in seeing people come and go, in seeing ego's rise
and fall, trust and mistrust, complaining and working
together in harmony. In seeing people saved, healed

and delivered from strongholds, and in seeing others leave the church unwilling to deal with the negative issues in their lives. In all of that and much more, one thing remains constant. God has a place for us, a secret place, and whoever chooses to dwell in that secret place will never fall away from God or family. Whoever abides in the secret place will always love, always trust, always forgive, and always persevere. The secret place is the "shadow of the Almighty." It is the very presence of God.

From Psalm 91 (Message Bible)

1-13   You who sit down in the High God's pres-
            ence, spend the night in Shaddai's shadow,
        Say this: "GOD, you're my refuge.
        I trust in you and I'm safe!"
        That's right—he rescues you from
            hidden traps,
        shields you from deadly hazards.
        His huge outstretched arms protect you—
            under them you're perfectly safe;
            his arms fend off all harm.

Whenever I have felt as though I couldn't go on, when I didn't want the struggle any longer, when I thought another job would be easier, I have always come back to that secret place in God's presence. You cannot find that place by striving. You cannot find that place by fleshly effort. You cannot find it by building a church building, by feeding the hungry, by visiting the homeless, or by being a Pastor of a church. In fact the ministries that we have are only truly successful if we first spend time in the secret place. It's a place that can be discovered in quietness. In simple trust and love for God. How can God search our hearts by His Spirit if we are always busy, always doing "His" works. After all, He is the only one who really knows how to accomplish "His" works, and we are created IN Christ Jesus unto good works.

Carol Arnott, Pastor John Arnott's wife, from the Toronto Airport Christian Fellowship, (AKA – The Toronto Blessing), has had some incredible experiences in the Lord. Their church has witnessed hundreds of thousands of visitors coming from all over the world, who have come to find healing and restoration in their souls. I was one of those people, and I heard Carol describe something that happened to her in the Spirit. She said that she was going to pray for people at the altar time, when she sensed the nudging of the Spirit to pray alone. She laid down on the floor and began to pray. She said that, after a few minutes she thought she'd better get up and pray for others. Just then, she described a sense of the Spirit touching her hands, and she thought she'd wait and see what happened. Over the next two hours, the Holy Spirit had filled her entire body, slowly and one phase at a time. Needless to say, she didn't spend much time praying with others on that day. She said to the Lord, "You could have done that all at once. Why did You take so much time?" Carol said the Lord replied, "It was because I wanted to spend time with you."

I have had many similar experiences. There must be a longing within us for closeness to God. If there is, you will not find it in working for God, but in the presence of His Spirit. "God is a Spirit, and they that worship Him must worship Him in spirit and in truth." The works that we do will be far more successful as we rest in Him and quit our striving. We need to give up our rights to get our way, and get back to trusting His love, trusting His plan for your life. The Word says - "He who began a good work in you, will be faithful to complete it."

Once, while preaching a tent revival in Nicaragua, I had finished my sermon and the altar was filled with about 300 people. I came off the platform thinking that I must touch and pray for every single person, and in order to do that I was going to have to act fast. I began touching people on the forehead very rapidly and quickly, saying a fast prayer, and moving to the next person. As I did this, I sensed an immediate rebuke from the Holy Spirit, saying "STOP THAT!" I stopped, and asked, "What would you have me to do Lord." The Spirit of God said to me, "I want you to love these people." I threw my arms around the next man I saw, and just held him, weeping in the presence of God. As I did, the Lord began to greatly touch Him. When I let go of Him I saw that God was touching everyone. I then began to move towards two teenage girls who were standing with their eyes closed a few feet away. As I moved towards them they just fell over in the Spirit of God right there on the dirt floor. I never touched them. God moved in that tent that night, by His power and love, and the Joy of the Lord filled everyone there. I didn't really have to do much, just love the people, tell them the truth, and be in love with Jesus. He did the rest.

Since God is love, ministry is as simple as loving people with God's love. Every believer in Christ has a gift, a talent, and a purpose that God has for you to fulfill, with the help and anointing of the Holy Spirit. The infilling of the Holy Spirit has several purposes. First it's important that we understand, according to scripture, that He (The Holy Spirit) is a person. He is the third person in the Godhead. God is one God, but in three persons, similar to the understanding that you and I have a body, a soul and a spirit.

Your body is your flesh, while your soul is made up of your mind, your will, and your emotions. Your spirit is your persona, that which drives you, and that which longs for relationship with God. It is my spirit that longs to connect with God in intimacy and relationship. It is my spirit that longs for God's Spirit to empower my soulish realm. Simply put, my soulish man (flesh) is attached to this world and the things that are in this world, but my spirit is willing and capable of connecting with God through His Spirit. Jesus once said to His disciples - "The spirit is willing, but the flesh is weak."

The fact is, we desperately need the infilling and empowering of the Holy Spirit every single day. Jesus said to Nicademas - "Flesh gives birth to flesh, but Spirit gives birth to spirit." Jesus also said, as multitudes followed him looking for more bread after he had fed over five thousand people miraculously - "Eat my flesh, and drink my blood.....Unless you eat my flesh and drink my blood, you have no life in you... The words I speak to you are spirit, and they are life." Most of the followers left Jesus at that time. Jesus then looked at His disciples and asked if they too would leave. They replied - "To whom shall we go, thou hast the words of life." While many people look to God for the meeting of their physical needs, God truly has much greater desires for us, than just meeting our physical needs. God says in Matthew chapter 6:33, not to worry about the food and the clothing, the physical things. He'll take care of that, but he says - "Seek first the kingdom of God, and His righteousness, and all these things will be added to you."

The desires that we have every day can be either driven by flesh, or by spirit. If your spirit is dead, your flesh will be greatly active in the desires and longings of this passing world. The simple key then is that we have an active moving of the Spirit of God within us, and that we have this moving of His Spirit within us often, daily, regularly, and continually. The effort that is required to accomplish this is that we seek Him. You and I can activate our human spirit's desire for God by putting ourselves in the proper position. Are you in position? Do you listen to music that induces your desire for God? Do you speak words of comfort or things that are demeaning of others? Do you judge others to justify yourself or forgive others because you know how much you need forgiveness? Do you have times every day, of shutting out your mundane activities for the purpose of igniting and infusing the Holy Spirit of God in you? This is extremely serious business. Without the

Holy Spirit's infilling and empowering, you have no weapons against the attacks of the enemy of your soul, Satan.

The way to get in position to be filled, led, and directed by the Spirit is simply to seek Him, and to be desperate for Him, and not worry about how your flesh may look. God doesn't want to give people a Holy Ghost experience just so that they can feel something, or experience something. God desires intimacy with us. He longs to be loved and sought after. He wants to know us, and for us to know Him. He will not know us, unless we open the door to His Spirit by drawing near to Him ("Draw near to God, and He will draw near to you").

I once went to a ministry conference in Toronto Canada, taking with me several leaders from our church. Our Youth Pastor's wife, Kerri, began to observe people behaving very strangely. She thought they were strange people. The reality was that they were not strange people, but they had become full to overflowing with the Holy Spirit. On the day of Pentecost the people of that day thought that the believers were drunk at 9 AM. When the Spirit of God is welcomed and invited to fill you, He will begin a work of healing, and that work will cause a physical manifestation in your body. The manifestation may seem strange, but the result is restored marriages, renewed minds, healed bodies, and lives that are suddenly and instantly finding direction, clarity, and deep, deep love; a love that they may have never thought possible.

As Kerri observed the people she began to jokingly make fun of some of them. Well, on the last day of the conference, there was Kerri, laying on the floor at the back of the sanctuary, with hands in the air, and seeking God for all of Him. As she prayed, she said, "Lord, if this is really you, would you touch my face." At that moment, as I had no idea what she was praying, the Holy Spirit said to me, "Reach down and touch Keri's face." I thought I should pray for her, but the Lord said, "No, just touch her face." I did, and what happened next was life altering for Kerri, as she began to cry, laugh, and roll on the floor. I tell you it doesn't matter how strange it may look, God is looking to put truth inside of you, and truth is life changing.

Kerri was unable to walk out of the building on her own that night, so we carried her out. As we left the building, she pointed at others who were in a similar state, saying, "I made fun of you, I'm sorry." Kerri Bovial was instrumental in deep intercessions for revival in our church after that. One night, very late, I had to run up to the church to get something I had left there. As I walked through the front door, I heard an unusual noise. It was the sound of deep intercession. Kerri was in the main sanctuary, crying out to God, all alone, late at night, and in a dark church sanctuary. Flesh will never lead a person this way, but when the Spirit of Jesus is given welcome entrance into a person's life, that person will find a new joy. That joy is in knowing, and walking in intimacy with the Savior, the Lord of Lords, and the King of all Kings. His name is Jesus, and I love Him.

Let's together hear the Word of God fresh and new again, and go after God as extravagant lovers of God. The third person of the Godhead, the Holy Spirit is waiting right now to fill you, heal you, renew you, restore you, and direct your steps, and He does all things well!

"ALL THINGS WORK TOGETHER FOR GOOD, TO THEM THAT LOVE GOD, TO THEM THAT ARE CALLED ACCORDING TO HIS PURPOSE."

ABOUT THE AUTHOR

T imothy Wiebe, along with his wife Rebekah, are
  the Senior Pastors of Harvest Assembly of God
Church in Georgetown, Texas. They have served
in full time ministry together since 1984 as Youth
Pastors, Assistant Pastors, Children's Pastors, Evangelists, and Senior Pastors. Timothy• and Rebekah
have taken the gospel across the US, and to other
parts of the world, such as the Island of Mauritius in
the Indian Ocean, Honduras and Nicaragua, singing
and preaching revival meetings, tent meetings, and
special services.

Timothy began testifying and preaching the Word
of God at the age of 16 after a life changing encounter
with the Lord at Calvary Temple Christian Center in
Springfield, Illinois in 1980. Under the tutelage of
Pastor Mark Johnson, Timothy grew in the Lord, grad-
uated from the church based High School, (Calvary
Academy), met and married his wife Rebekah, and

they began their life and ministry together. Timothy is a graduate of Berean University.

The message that burns strongest on Timothy's heart is that God longs to have intimate fellowship with anyone who will call on Him. That Jesus took our sins, and longs to bring people into covenant relationship with Him, and that through the power and presence of the Holy Spirit, people from any type of history or background can live victoriously, with joy and with great peace.

Timothy's messages of hope and deliverance can be heard via the Internet, by going to www.harvest-churchaog.org and clicking on "Online Sermons."

To contact the author, please write:
Timothy Wiebe
6040 Airport Road
Georgetown, Texas 78628
Or call: (512-863-0854)

CPSIA information can be obtained
at www.ICGtesting.com
Printed in the USA
LVHW072117260623
750830LV00001B/52